FURNITURE FINISHING

BY THE SAME AUTHOR

How to Finish off Your Basement or Attic
101 Free Plans for the Handy Home-owner
One Hundred & One Projects for Bottle Cutters
Decks
Carpentry

FURNITURE FINISHING

W. I. FISCHMAN

Drawings by Lloyd Birmingham

BOBBS-MERRILL
Indianapolis/New York

FIRST PRINTING

Designed by Bernard Schleifer
Manufactured in the United States of America

Library of Congress Cataloging in Publication Data

Fischman, Walter Ian.
   Furniture finishing.

   Includes index.
   1. Furniture finishing.   I. Title.
TT199.4.F47   684.1′043   78-55663
ISBN 0-672-52349-3

To my friend Everett C. (Bud) Johnson,
for whom fine wood, magnificent craftsmanship
and beautiful finishing
have a very special meaning

CONTENTS

Part I
The Basics

FINISHES AND OTHER MATERIALS 1

OVER THE YEARS, quite a complicated mystique has developed about the various steps in finishing or refinishing furniture. Don't believe it for a moment. The work is easy. Since you can take it in steps or stages, you can plan the job around your own schedule so that you need not get tired or bored. There is just one important precaution: The first few times you try any of the finishing schedules in this book, follow the instructions exactly. Do not introduce any ideas of your own. Later, when you have the how-to down perfectly, you can try your own variations. And good luck to you.

Also, don't be scared off by any of the techniques that the old-time craftsmen were supposed to have learned over years and years of apprenticeship. Granted, in those long-departed days, they may have tackled finishing in a more complicated way. Certainly they had none of the tools and materials at our disposal today. But much of the laborious work has been trimmed, thanks to a series of breakthroughs in research laboratories, and with just a bit of experience under your belt you will be able to handle today's versions of those very same routines. And you will get beautiful results in a fraction of the time.

There is one other important factor. No matter how rough and ready the project, you are still working with the feel of the wood. You are a craftsman—not a mere mechanic. With the variety of wood tones and colors available to you, you have an easy opportunity to create something beautiful, perhaps even an heirloom for the future.

THE BASIC FINISHES

There are only a few basic types of finishes. Of course there is a huge number of variations that fall somewhere in between, but the techniques for using them are virtually the same as for the primary finishes listed below. No matter how they verge and merge, they are all offshoots of the same basic materials. You will be picking and choosing from only a handful of reliable finishes.

If there is a trick to selecting the proper finish for a particular project, it's this: Know the final effect you are seeking—antique, sleek-modern, carefree, high-gloss, colorful. Have it fixed in your mind before you begin work. Once you have made this decision, the rest is merely a matter of getting there, and that's what this book is all about.

Shellac

If you are refinishing an antique and want to make the new surface match the original tone as closely as possible, you may very well decide to use shellac. It's a traditional finish that's been popular for hundreds of years.

From a how-to standpoint, shellac has much in its favor. It is easy to apply and dries with incredible swiftness (much of the liquid is alcohol). This means you will be able to apply several coats, one on top of the other, without long drying periods in between. Also important is the fact that this finish is most forgiving about such minor mistakes as brush marks, runs or sags. It has a tendency to level off and hide most signs of amateur brushwork.

Unfortunately, it does leave a great deal to be desired in the area of durability. Both water and alcohol stain it quite badly. Also, it has little resistance to abrasion, so that scratches leave behind visible reminders in the form of white streaks. As you can see, it is not a wise choice if you have a relaxed, casual attitude about your surroundings and the entertaining you do in your home. Rough-and-tumble it's not.

Varnish

If you are looking for durability, varnish is for you. This coating is known for its tough surface. Some types of varnish are even resistant to weather; after all, they are used on boats. In addition, this finish is both alcohol- and waterproof. You can buff it to a nice soft sheen or select a varnish that will dry to a hard, slick gloss.

Varnish is not easy to apply. For the most part, it is slow-drying; you have to be especially careful not to allow dust particles and the like to settle on the surface before it hardens. Brush marks are definitely a problem and will show up, along with an assortment of bubbles, unless you have perfected your application technique.

There is something formal about a varnish finish, perhaps because it forms a definite layer or "skin" on the surface. So, from a decorating standpoint, it looks a little out of place as a finish for casual furniture. On the other hand, if you are willing to take the time required for a hard, durable finish, this might be the ideal choice for furniture that will receive a great deal of abuse in the course of day-to-day living.

Lacquer

When you think of contemporary finishes, lacquer is probably the first that comes to mind. It's as up-to-date as today, and is perfect for sleek, modern furniture. The appearance of the surface will be quite in tune with the styling of the chairs and tables. Although it is not so weatherproof as some kinds of varnish, you still can use it to protect outdoor furniture from rain and inclement weather.

Lacquer is probably the clearest of all coatings that you can apply to any wood surface. Although it forms a definite "skin" on top of the wood, it retains the natural tone of the wood more nearly than does any other finish. This does not mean that it will protect the surface without causing any color changes at all; even water applied to wood will darken it. However, lacquer will retain the lightest possible tones. As a knock-about finish in households where the living is casual, lacquer has the added advantage of being totally impervious to alcohol, water and many other common household liquids. It dries to a super-high gloss and allows the delicate gradations of wood grain to show through.

Lacquer can be applied with either brush or spray. Just make sure you match the method of application to the particular type of lacquer you have purchased. Spraying lacquer dries too fast for brushwork, and the brushing variety is too thick for proper coating by a spray gun. Application is easy, as lacquer levels well to cover any mistakes.

One more point: Despite the talk of a crystal-clear surface, lacquer comes in many colors, including some of the brilliant, vibrant tones that are popular today. Somehow even black lacquer looks jazzy, perhaps because of the glossy surface.

Polyurethane

Originally developed in the lab as a scuff-proof, wear-resistant coating for flooring, polyurethane is now much in demand as a furniture finish. It is probably the toughest coating you can brush onto a piece of wood. When completely dry, it is resistant to practically anything you can find in the house, including of course alcohol, water and household cleaners.

Polyurethane finishes are applied with a brush. Although drying time varies, most brands set dust-free in a relatively short time— certainly far more quickly than varnish. The coating is designed to be self-leveling, so that brush marks, thick spots and the like tend to even out as it dries.

The finish is built up in several layers to form a definite surface coating. When it was first introduced, this finish was available only in glossy format. You can now also buy it with a dull finish. If you have the glossy type and want a dull finish, you will need to steel-wool the last layer. This is a complicated procedure, since the timing is fairly critical. You have to wait until the finish has hardened but has not reached the final stage of tautness. If you wait too long before using steel wool, the finish just shrugs off the metal fibers.

Although not so clear as lacquer, the clear polyurethane imparts only a slightly deeper tone. Use it wherever you are seeking a high-gloss surface that's chemical resistant and tough enough to take most household rough-and-tumble.

Penetrating sealer

You'll find this finish under various brand names, but the term "penetrating sealer" will get you what you want at most hardware and paint stores across the country. As the name indicates, this coating is designed to soak into the wood. It actually goes below the surface and toughens the wood fibers. Because of this, a penetrating-sealer finish has one unique quality: It will preserve the feel and texture of the wood. If you are building utility cabinets out of second-grade fir plywood, this may not be a particularly desirable quality. On the other hand, if you are finishing furniture made of woods that have a nice touch-quality, such as oak, walnut, or any of the other fine cabinet woods, you have the opportunity to add another dimension to your work.

Surprisingly enough, penetrating sealer is also rugged. Like polyurethane, it was originally designed for floors. It's available in clear (which actually gives you a slight amber tint) as well as in various natural tints that add different hues to the finished surface.

In addition to durability, the material has one other gigantic plus: It is an absolute snap to apply. You can brush it on, swab it on, or pour it on. The only requirement is to get the wood surface to absorb as much of the finish as possible. Of course the process is done in layers, with drying time in between, but it is still so easy that you will never begrudge the breathing time. Its only real disadvantage is that it does not form a skin on top of the wood surface.

Penetrating sealer makes a superb base for a wax finish, if you want the final effect to be a soft luster. Used by itself without the wax, it is resistant to most household chemicals and alcohol.

Wax

For the warm, mellow effect wax can impart, there is no finish that can beat it. It seems as if good wood has a natural affinity for well-rubbed wax. The application process is ease itself. No tricks, no difficult techniques; the only drawback is labor. To get a really good wax finish you must do a lot of buffing. And don't think just one good polishing session will do the trick; for a really topflight finish, you will have to wipe on a new layer of wax at regular intervals and then buff it.

If you are refinishing or restoring an antique piece, you may have no other choice than to use a wax finish. This used to be the most popular surfacing material, and an authentic restoration may simply call for more of the same. However, there are rewards. As the thin, well-buffed layers of wax build up on the surface, they also seem to seep down into the wood and add a transparency. After a while a properly applied wax finish develops a depth, or patina, that is impossible to duplicate by any other means.

Of course, a lot depends on the wax you use. Considering all the effort involved, it pays to apply nothing but cabinetmaker's paste wax. This comes in clear as well as stained tones. If you don't want to do all the work by hand, you can use a power-buffer. This is a round fiber brush that hooks onto the chuck of an electric drill. It not only removes the excess wax from the surface, but it also drives the material down into the pores of the wood. At the same time it gives a soft sheen to the surface.

When putting a wax finish on new or completely stripped wood, penetrating sealer is a perfect undercoat. Build up a couple of layers of this material before starting to apply wax. The final finish will be tougher, and the depth of the glow will appear even deeper. One thing to remember about wax is that it is not durable. Moisture will stain it, and it is easily marred.

Enamel

Enamel is simply a glossy colored paint, and for many purposes it makes a perfect finish. It is opaque, so it covers all sorts of tonal variations in the wood, as well as stains and other imperfections. It can be cleaned. It will also hide even large-scale repairs to the undersurface, as well as the usual assortment of plastic wood patches. There is a rainbow-hued palette available, so that you can match the finish to virtually any decorating scheme in the house. Available in either a semi- or high-gloss finish, most enamel is generally tough enough to shrug off the stains of alcohol, water, and ordinary household preparations. Of course it is possible to chip or scratch it, but it is fairly durable and stands up well to wear.

In contemporary decorating schemes, enamel is a familiar sight in many children's rooms, where the bright colors add a cheerful note; and it is often used in other rooms to create color accents. Individual pieces of furniture or a small grouping can be painted in a bright modern color to create a focal point.

Originally, enamel was a finicky finish to apply. No more. Gone are the days when brush marks or other signs of an amateur hand spoiled the finished effect. As long as you are reasonably careful in applying a fairly even layer of paint, the final surface will be smooth, flat, and nearly perfect.

Oil

Oil is probably the most overrated material in the furniture-finishing field. And the most impractical is linseed oil. In blunt terms: No one should use this as a finish on furniture. In view of all the effective, easy-to-apply finishes currently available, linseed oil makes absolutely no sense. Granted, it is spoken of in hushed tones as the true craftsman's method, but don't you believe it for a moment; this is sheer nonsense. Linseed oil goes on easily—and eventually dries to a sticky, messy finish.

"Ah," you say. "All that applies to straight linseed oil. How about boiled linseed oil?" Well, it's a little better, but not much. It just takes more time for it to reach the messy, tacky stage. So remove this coating from your list. The only guarantee you get from it is trouble.

There are some new types of oil finishes that are supposed to avoid this unhappy situation. However, if you will read the label carefully, you will generally find that they are a variation of penetrating sealer—with a bit of oil added to the formula. The dire words above do not apply to this particular material. It has most of the properties and many of the advantages of penetrating sealer. The oil in the formula adds some additional tonal value if you happen to like that effect. Do be very careful, however, to read the label before you apply the coating.

OTHER MATERIALS YOU WILL USE

There are other materials that are essential in some finishing schedules. Although these will be covered in more detail later, here's a brief description of each.

Filler

As the name indicates, filler is used to fill in hollows in the grain of the wood. While some very close grained woods don't need it, others have a more open surface (oak, for example) where there are miniature craters that must be filled in to create a level surface. For the most part, using filler is simple: Wipe it on and wipe it off.

Stain

Much of the beauty of a wood finish comes from the tones and hues that you give it. Sad to say, even fine cabinet woods such as oak, walnut, teak or mahogany can be drab. Quite often it's necessary to add the deeper, richer hues usually associated with these woods in the form of stain.

Stain can also be used in a more devious way. Through the use of stain, an inexpensive wood can sometimes be disguised to look like fine cabinet lumber. Properly done, the transformation can be highly effective.

Then, too, some wood is just plain dull. Without the addition of stain, its surface is so bland that it might just as well be composition board. In such a case, stain can add the extra element of excitement needed to lift the whole effect out of the humdrum.

Bleach

Bleach is just the opposite of stain. Instead of adding color, it removes it. Bleach can also lighten wood, which is a must for a blond finish and for many natural finishes. It is also useful for removing stains. Frequently, in stripping an old piece of furniture, you will find dark areas in the wood that penetrate so deeply that it is impossible to remove them with sandpaper. In many instances, these spots can be lightened to match the rest of the wood through the use of bleach.

The process is a simple one: Apply the bleach, allow it time to work, and then brush it off or neutralize it.

EQUIPMENT AND WORKING CONDITIONS 2

EQUIPMENT

EXCEPT FOR A large stack of newspapers and plenty of clean, dry rags, there are relatively few materials needed for furniture finishing. But it is important that the tools you use be precisely suited to the job. If you are in doubt about what equipment to buy, rely on the advice of the man behind the counter at the paint or hardware store. Although they are a fast-vanishing breed, there still seem to be a few hardware or paint store owners who know their business and are willing to impart trade secrets they've learned over the years. If you're lucky enough to find such an individual, by all means try to establish a teacher-pupil relationship. You have found a gem indeed.

The choice of equipment is indeed an area where the old carpenter's adage can be applied: Even a careful workman is only as good as his tools. There is really no excuse for starting the job improperly equipped. Even the most expensive items, such as a top-quality natural bristle brush, will return value many times over in terms of service rendered.

Brushes

A good-quality brush is designed to be used over and over again. Since a wood surface is not very abrasive, it won't wear down the bristles. Unless you are trying to paint concrete, the brush will stay in good shape for quite some time. Therefore, if you think of the purchase price as being extended over many, many years of use, that initial cost is not so high. Added to this is the fact that there is a "feel" to a top-quality brush that can never be duplicated by an inexpensive imitation.

Immediately following those words designed to lead you into buying quality materials, it is time to waffle a bit on this same question. There are some craftsmen, professionals included, who seriously advocate the use of a cheap disposable brush. Here is their thinking: In order to use a brush a second, third or hundredth time, you must clean it thoroughly. Admittedly, cleaning brushes is a messy, dull task that is much easier to handle in slapdash fashion. But unless the brush is perfectly clean, it will not perform correctly the next time. The bristles won't hold paint properly or release the coating smoothly, and bits and pieces of the old accumulated material are likely to flow out and become embedded in the new surface.

To get around this, some craftsmen are willing to forego the smoothness and performance of a top-quality brush. They'll settle for a lesser quality tool and simply toss it out after it's used. This is a choice you will have to make for yourself, based on your own work habits and requirements.

The signs of quality in a brush are relatively easy to spot. Hold the brush up to a good light and fan out the bristles. Take a close look at the tips. They should be "flagged," or frayed and split. Those shabby-looking tips retain the paint when you dunk the brush in the coating and then allow it to flow out smoothly onto the surface.

In the early days of synthetic bristle brushes, the ends of the bristles were roughened but not flagged. As a result the bristles dripped paint at unexpected times. If this has been your experience and you have therefore become soured on the idea of synthetic bristles, better give the product a second look. This problem has now been completely overcome. You'll find it hard to distinguish between natural and nylon bristles.

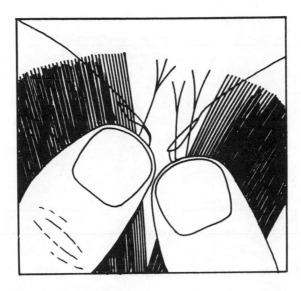

Fig. 1.   Brush with flagged bristles.

Make certain the brush has bristles of the proper length. This is a subjective quality, but it contributes to the "feel" of the brush. It is the length of the bristles that gives the brush a springiness and imparts a smoothness to the back-and-forth action.

At the store, hold the brush as if you were actually using it, and brush the bristles back and forth across the back of your hand. There should be life to the action. This is hard to describe, but you will spot it immediately; or rather, you will be able to detect the reverse. A dead brush feels exactly as the word implies; there is no spring or resilience to the bristles. Any kind of refinishing job with such a brush is almost guaranteed to be a total disaster.

Make certain the bristles are firmly fixed to the ferrule (the metal band or base around the brush); spread them apart so you can see how they are attached. Work the brush back and forth across your hand to see if any loose bristles come out. Don't be dismayed if you get one or two, but don't buy any brush that seems to be losing them in a wholesale manner.

The bristles of a good brush are arranged in a slight flare, so that they are wider at the tip than at the handle. They should also be tapered at the end to form a wedge shape.

When you fan open the bristles, you will notice that there is a

Fig. 2. Brush with tapered tip.

wooden wedge in the center. This is standard construction, but the wedge should not be too thick. If it is, the lower bristles on either side will be thin. A brush with a wide wedge in the center and consequently fewer bristles on the sides will not hold as much paint, nor can it be used in so smooth a fashion.

Finally, examine the brush to see if care has been taken in the smoothing and finishing of the handle. Obviously, this won't affect the working of the brush itself, but it does tell you something about the general manufacturing quality. Your best bet is to stick with quality products made by well-known companies.

Rollers

Surprisingly enough, you can use rollers with some finishing materials. The list of don'ts, however, is longer than the acceptable list. Don't try to use a roller with shellac, varnish, or lacquer. Either you will introduce too many bubbles, or the coating will gum up the roller. However, some types of paint and enamel finishes, as well as such items as penetrating sealer, can be quite successfully applied with a roller. Just make sure that you have the proper tool for the job. In most instances, this means a foam-cylinder roller, but check the instructions on the container of the particular finish you are using.

If you opt to use a roller, be sure to try it and the finish on scrap wood before you start a full-scale project. Also make sure that you can properly clean the roller cylinder, or that it is inexpensive enough so that you can merely toss it out after each coat.

Tack cloth

As the name indicates, a tack cloth is a piece of cloth that's been specially treated to make it slightly sticky or tacky. This simple bit of equipment, properly used, can be your key to an absolutely perfect finish. Although you can buy ready-to-use tack cloths in most paint and hardware stores, they are so inexpensive and easy to make that a purchase hardly seems worthwhile. Here's how. (Incidentally, it's a good idea to make several at one time. Stored in a screw-topped jar, they will remain in usable condition almost indefinitely.)

A well-washed diaper works best, but you can use almost any soft, lint-free cloth that has been washed often enough so that all of the starch and sizing are out of it. Soak the cloth in water and then wring it out thoroughly. Immediately saturate the cloth with turpentine. Once more, squeeze and wring the cloth until it is still wet but doesn't drip. Open it out and dribble varnish (any kind of varnish will do) onto it until the fabric is pretty well speckled with it. Roll the cloth, and wring it out firmly once again. The idea is to distribute the varnish in a thin, even coating. Open up the cloth, refold, and rewring until the varnish seems to be evenly distributed. If necessary, add a little bit more varnish and repeat the process. The final result should be a piece of moist cloth that has a slightly sticky feel without being gummy or adhesive in any way.

Picking stick

A picking stick is another simple tool that's well described by its name, since you use it to pick loose material from your finish. Once you've made and used this handy accessory, you'll wonder how you ever got along without it. To make picking sticks, gather together several slivers of wood about as big around as a wooden matchstick and eight to ten inches long. Bamboo cocktail skewers are perfect for this. You also need some crushed or powdered rosin. Sometimes paint or hardware stores carry this item, but if yours doesn't, head for your nearest sporting goods store or music store. At the sporting goods store, buy a rosin

Fig. 3. Making a picking stick.

bag—the kind used by baseball players to help their fingers grip the ball firmly. Once you have cut open the fabric, you'll find a more than ample supply of rosin inside. Music stores carry rosin in the form of a block; violin players need it to coat bow strings. In this case you'll have to pound the rosin until it's reduced to a powder.

Improvise a double boiler by putting a small can (one used for cocktail spreads is excellent) into a larger pot full of water. Measure out your ingredients: approximately one part of varnish (again, any kind of varnish) to eight parts of rosin. Put the varnish into the small can. Bring the water to a boil, and gradually add the rosin to the varnish, stirring carefully all the time. It's like making candy, and the test for doneness is pretty much the same. Dip the tip of a stick into the mixture. When the rosin and varnish mixture forms a small, gummy ball on the end of the stick, it's done. One at a time, dip the sticks into the mixture. Wet your fingers, and shape each ball into a smooth, compact mass. Keep it small. Then tap and roll the ball against the palm of your hand until it becomes firm and definitely sticky.

As with the tack cloths, it's a good idea to make several picking sticks at one time. You can store them in any kind of tall, screw-topped jar; the kind that fancy olives come in is perfect for this purpose.

How to use a tack cloth and a picking stick

A tack cloth is intended for the last, final cleanup before you apply a finish. After the surface has been completely sanded, after it has been wiped thoroughly with a dry cloth, after it has been vacuumed, use a tack cloth as the final step. Merely wipe the surface with it. You will be amazed to discover that there is still a fine layer of dust on what appeared to be an absolutely clean surface. The tack cloth will pick up this layer and hold it, so you can thus remove the last bit of dirt from the surface.

Also use the tack cloth if a finish is to be sanded or steel-wooled between layers. The procedure is the same. After repeated wiping and vacuuming, go over the entire surface with the tack cloth. Do not use it as the first step in any clean-up job. Its sticky surface will simply load up with sawdust and it will be unusable. However, for that final touch, it will stay in shape for quite some time. Between uses, keep the tack cloth stored in a glass jar with a tightly fitting screw cap. If the tack cloth appears to be losing its pick-up quality or is becoming loaded with dust, you can rejuvenate it by rinsing it out in water and sprinkling more varnish on it, followed by the folding and wringing routine.

A picking stick is designed to remove a single, loose brush bristle or speck of dirt from the surface of a newly finished piece. If you have ever applied a careful, smooth finish and then checked the result to find a single hair embedded, you'll know just how dismaying this problem can be. Furthermore, if you've ever tried to pick out the hair, using a brush or your fingertips, you also know how disastrous the results can be. A picking stick is perfect for this job. Properly used, it will pick up the single imperfection from the surface while creating the least possible disturbance to the freshly applied finish.

Surprisingly enough, there is a special technique for using this simple tool. Do not try to pick up a brush bristle with a sweeping or jabbing motion. This will just make a big mar in the finish. Instead, very lightly touch the sticky tip of the stick to the loose bristle. Immediately lift the stick straight up. The bristle will stick to the tip. If the finish is still wet enough for more brushwork, you can smooth over the slight mark left by the hair. If not, leave it alone, sand or steel-wool the surface when it is completely dry, and apply new finish on top.

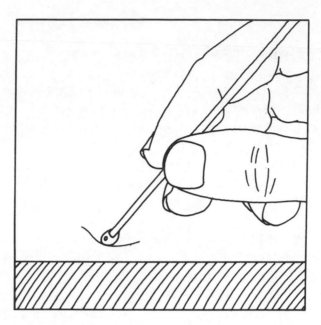

Fig. 4.   Using a picking stick.

Other equipment

For some finishes, you will need to use other tools and equipment. These will be discussed in later chapters. For example, spray guns are covered in chapter 11; abrasives such as sandpaper and steel wool are covered in chapter 5.

WORK AREA

Ideally, the best spot for doing furniture finishing is a sheltered porch in a warm climate. This obviously restricts the project to a limited number of people in a narrow segment of the country. Most of us have to work under less than ideal conditions. However, if you choose your work area carefully, you should have absolutely no problems.

Ventilation

Many coatings and removers contain ingredients that can cause headache, nausea, or eye irritation. This is true even of those supposed to be "safe." If the fumes are concentrated, they can be anything from unpleasant to dangerous. For this reason, make sure there is plenty of ventilation. If you are working indoors, this can be in the form of a small low-speed fan at an open window pulling air out, plus another open window on the other side of the room. The main idea is to get a gentle current of air flowing slowly through the entire area. A whirlwind is unnecessary and undesirable; it will just create more dust to settle on the surface.

Space

No matter how carefully organized you are, furniture finishing is a project that always seems to spread out. Allow yourself as much room as possible. The job is much easier if you have work space on all sides.

Moisture control

If the area where you are working is damp, the finish will not dry properly. By the same token, if you are working outside in direct sunlight, the finish is likely to dry so quickly that you won't be able to smooth it properly. As work areas, basements are fine as long as they are reasonably dry; but in general, furniture finishing is a more reliable process when done aboveground.

OTHER CONSIDERATIONS

Organization

Gather all the materials you will need before you start the job. Check over the list carefully before you begin. There are very few finishing schedules that allow enough slack time for you to run over to the paint store to buy the materials you forgot to pick up originally.

Until the finishing routine becomes second nature to you, actually write out a schedule and fasten it to the wall. If necessary, tick off each stage with a pencil mark as you go.

Information

This next bit of instruction is so simple it's almost ludicrous, yet not following it is probably the single most common cause of failure in furniture finishing today. The words belong in capital letters: READ THE LABEL.

If you haven't taken the time for this informative procedure in quite a few years, you are in for a pleasant surprise. In the old days, the labels on finishing materials were intended for knowledgeable professionals only, so in very terse fashion they listed the precise percentage of pigment, vehicle, base, et cetera. All that has changed. Manufacturers have redesigned their containers to attract the new cadre of do-it-yourselfers. These days, labels will not only tell you exactly what's inside the container but will also give detailed, specific advice on applying the contents. Follow these instructions exactly. Later—much later—when you have established your own success record, you can vary the instructions according to your own ideas. For now, do not inject any of your own.

Fire

Although the trend is toward nonflammable finishes, this goal has not yet been reached. Many finishing materials are highly flammable, especially when brushed or sprayed onto a wide area. For safety's sake, do not smoke while applying a finish. If you are working in the kitchen, shut off (do not blow out) the pilot light on the stove. Do not work in a furnace room in the heating season when the pilot light for that appliance will be on. Buy and keep at hand a small reliable fire extinguisher; either the carbon dioxide type or the type that uses a dry powder dispersed under pressure seems to work best. The advantage of the carbon dioxide type over all the others is that the fire quenching will not damage the finish.

Skin irritation

Everyone's skin is different, and everyone reacts in a different manner to almost every substance, but by now you should have a good idea of how your skin will react to most common chemicals. If you have any tendency at all to break out in a rash or red blotches, take extra precautions when finishing furniture. Wear disposable gloves. Cover your arms with a long-sleeved shirt. Wear a hat.

Eye protection

It's surprisingly easy to flick a bit of paint onto your face, and it can be quite unpleasant if it gets into your eyes. For any finish that can be irritating or has a warning to this effect on the label, be sure to wear simple plastic goggles. You can buy these at most paint and hardware stores. They are comfortable to wear and are certainly worth any minor inconvenience to save you from eye irritation.

Inhalation of fumes

There is no real protection against inhaling irritating fumes, except for providing plenty of ventilation. If in spite of this you find that a particular finish is especially irritating to breathe when you work, better switch to some other finishing procedure. You can buy small, inexpensive filter masks at most paint and hardware stores, but these are effective only for actual particles of paint. Definitely use a mask while spraying a coating, but don't expect it to be effective against irritating fumes.

Materials

Except for some staples such as turpentine and wax, your best bet is to buy only the quantities needed for each specific job. Accumulating all sorts of containers with a bit of material in the bottom of each one is worthless and frustrating. The stuff is never usable when you need it. Instead, start each job with fresh materials, and toss out the dribs and drabs that remain when you have finished. If you do want to preserve some of the original material for touch-ups, transfer it to a small container that you can fill right up to the brim. Seal it carefully. Baby food jars are the craftman's old standby for this purpose.

One final thought: Always have plenty of soft, clean, dry rags on hand for wiping and cleaning. Of course any experienced craftsman will tell you this is nonsense: There is no such thing as having enough rags.

Part II
Preparing for the New Finish

MINOR REPAIRS 3

FOR THE MOST PART, minor repairs to furniture fall into two general categories: the work you do to stave off a major refinishing project, mostly spot repairs; and the type of work you do when you are already committed to a complete refinishing schedule—such as tightening wobbly chair legs, refitting drawers, and "unwarping" tabletops. If you are lucky, the particular piece of furniture you are working on won't need more than one or two repairs. However, eventually you will come upon the inevitable piece of furniture that requires nearly every trick in the book. Don't be discouraged. Despite the fact that it may seem like a terrifyingly large amount of work at the outset, it really is not. Even large-scale projects consist of a series of simple repairs.

REMOVING MINOR MARS WITHOUT REFINISHING

Scratches

A scratch is really two mars combined. There is a minute gouge in the surface of the finish, and at the same time there is also a change of color. So repairing a scratch takes a combined approach.

Fig. 5. Using iodine to repair a scratch in a mahogany surface.

The first step is to stain the scratch back to something approximating the original color. You can use several materials for this job. If the wood is walnut, try rubbing the scratch with a freshly shelled walnut meat. That's not so strange as it sounds. The nut contains a dark oil that will color the exposed surface to a shade close to the original.

In the case of mahogany, try ordinary iodine from the medicine cabinet. Wrap a tiny wisp of cotton around the end of a toothpick to make an applicator. Using this as a daubing brush, coat the scratch.

Use this same technique to apply a tiny line of paint to a scratch in an enameled tabletop. If the surface is the product of a previous project, you might have some of the original finish around. If not, mix a batch to get as close to the color as possible.

For other finishes, you can experiment with varnish, colors, and other types of pigments that will sometimes work.

Although scratch sticks are sold in most hardware and paint stores under a wide variety of names, these crayon-like gadgets are nothing more than colored wax. However, they can sometimes do a fairly presentable job in hiding small scratches and toning down larger ones. To use them, merely rub them back and forth across the scratch (not paral-

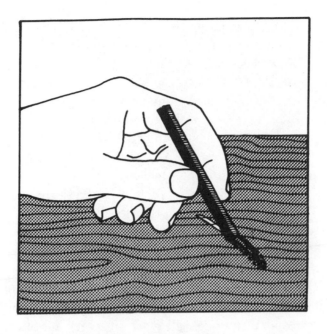

Fig. 6. Rub the scratch stick across the scratch.

Fig. 7. Remove the excess wax with stiff cardboard.

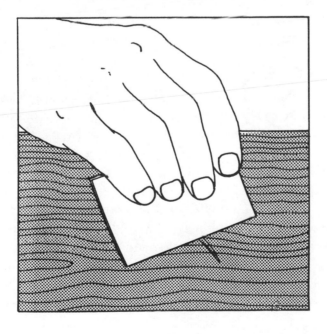

lel with it). The idea is to fill up the little crevice. Try to choose a color that matches the original finish. If this is impossible, you can sometimes blend two or three sticks by using them one after another to achieve an in-between shade. And don't be afraid to try ordinary crayons. They will work too, in a surprisingly large number of cases.

When working with any of the colored wax sticks, after you have filled in the scratch, use a piece of stiff fiberboard or cardboard to scrape the excess material off the surface. Work with a light touch so that you don't make more scratches in the process.

Finally, wipe on a thin coat of paste wax and buff-polish the spot. Don't be too liberal with wax. A too-thick coating has a tendency to lift the colored wax from the scratch, and you might have to start all over again.

Important note: Almost all of these techniques for removing scratches should be approached on a trial-and-error basis. Since there is a huge variety of available finishes, goods and materials, it stands to reason that no one technique will work in every instance. For this reason, it's a good idea to test all procedures in an inconspicuous spot first. If there is a scratch on the top surface of a table, you don't want to do your experimenting in plain view. Turn the table over. If necessary make a small scratch on the underside, and then check your covering technique.

Alcohol rings

Surprisingly enough, alcohol rings look vastly more serious than they really are. You see, the white ring left by a forgotten glass doesn't actually penetrate the finish. Most of the damage is right on the surface. For this reason, it can usually be washed away by using a very mild abrasive.

No need to scurry over to the paint store. Instead, make a paste from cigarette ash and lemon juice. You'll need only a very small amount. Dip a soft cloth into this mixture and then very gently rub the alcohol ring with it. The result will be twofold. Cigarette ash is actually a very fine abrasive, so it will wear away a minute amount of the surface. At the same time, lemon juice, a fairly mild bleach, will remove any remaining discoloration. Stop immediately when the alcohol ring is gone. Using a damp cloth, clean off all remnants of ash and lemon juice.

Fig. 8.   Washing away an alcohol ring with cigarette ash and lemon juice.

Dry the spot; then wax and polish it, with lots of buffing. If you've done the work carefully, the repair will be virtually imperceptible.

Cigarette burns

Cigarette burns are serious, and the repair is considerably more involved. The heat from the cigarette actually chars the surface. If the mar is truly serious, it can go right through the finish and char the wood underneath. In any event, the repair technique is the same.

Using a sharp knife blade, carefully scrape away the damaged finish; if necessary, scrape the wood too. Remove all traces of charred material.

If you had to scrape away wood, then start by rebuilding with wood putty. Use the type that's mixed with water. Apply it carefully, rebuilding the scraped area until it is as nearly level as possible with the surface of the wood (the wood, not the finish). Allow the putty to dry thoroughly, and then sand it smooth. Using wood stain and a small brush, tint the putty until it matches the wood. You may not be able to

Fig. 9. Scraping away the damage from a cigarette burn.

do a perfect job here, but at least come as close as you can. If you use the ready-mixed cellulose-type filler, or plastic wood, for this job (it smells like banana oil and dries quite quickly), use a tinted type that matches the tone of the finished surface well. This material does not accept many types of stain, so you won't have the opportunity of matching the color as you would with the water-mixed putty.

After the putty is dry and stained, start building up the surface in that one spot, duplicating the original finish as closely as possible. If it's shellac, use shellac; if varnish, then varnish. It will probably take quite a few layers, and be sure to allow sufficient drying time in between. When you have finally built up the finish in the marred area until it is level with the surface of the original finish, blend in the repair. For this job, use extra-fine steel wool loaded with paste wax. Work back and forth across the surface in the direction of the grain. Then wax and polish the area, and buff well. If you matched the shading and tone of the finish reasonably well, the repaired area should be nearly invisible.

Loose veneer

You can blame it on today's steam-heated homes, but whatever the cause, the problem of loose veneer can be downright annoying. Generally, the combination of excessive moisture followed by periods of dry heat takes a terrible toll on veneered furniture. You will notice the damage first at the edges, where the veneer has started to work loose from the surface of the wood underneath. If you repair the damage at the start, when the trouble is confined to a small area, you probably will stave off a major repair job later.

The problem is always the same. The glue that holds the veneer to the base underneath has disintegrated and no longer does the job. This makes the repair a little complicated, because the solution depends on the type of glue. If the piece of furniture is an antique, or at least more than forty or fifty years old, the chances are that some form of animal- or fish-based adhesive was used to attach the veneer. Very carefully lift the loose veneer and peer underneath. Wet a finger, and if possible press the tip against the underside of the veneer. If the glue gets tacky, the

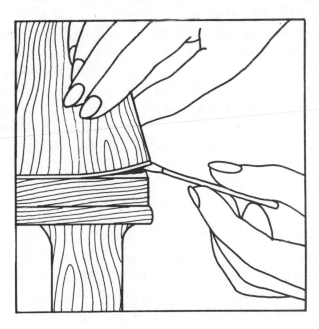

Fig. 10. Try to repair loose veneer by moistening the dried-out glue underneath.

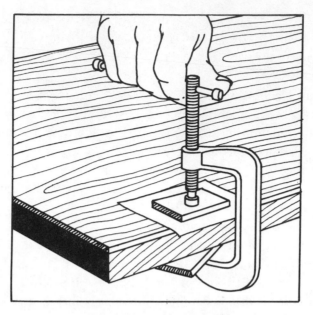

Fig. 11. Hold the veneer in position with a C-clamp.

repair will be easy. You have learned that the glue is probably animal-based and that it's water soluble. You have also learned that there's enough of it still in place to be reactivated.

Wet a cotton swab or some paper towels and work them underneath the veneer as far back into the crevice as you can without damaging the surface. If necessary add more water with an eye dropper. The whole idea is to soften the glue that remains so that it will stick fast again. Pull out the paper towels and check to see if the glue is sticky. If it is, just press the loose flap of veneer back into position. Cover the surface with a couple of layers of wax paper and a flat board. Tighten down the veneer with a C-clamp (be sure to pad the other end of the clamp, too, so that you don't damage the underside of the furniture top).

Quite frankly, this maneuver may not work. However, it's worth a try, because it is a relatively easy shortcut. If it doesn't work, here's another remedy.

If the glue did become sticky when you moistened it but didn't keep the veneer down in position, it is probably some form of fish or animal glue. The only trouble is that there isn't enough of it. So in order to make a permanent repair, you should add some more glue. Be very careful, however. Different types of glue do not blend well. To be on the

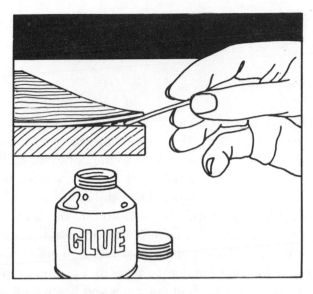

Fig. 12. Applying new glue with a sliver of wood.

safe side, work some hide glue (it's the most generally available type of animal glue) into the crevice. Use a sliver of wood to coat the surface all the way back. Then cover and clamp in exactly the same way. Wipe off any excess that oozes out before it has a chance to get hard.

Many paint stores, some of the old-time hardware stores, and almost all cabinetmaker supply houses sell liquid hide glue. It's a brownish runny paste that comes in a squeeze tube.

If you're not sure about the type of glue that was originally used to hold down the veneer, or if you can't get any hide glue, there is another solution. If you want to be daring, add some modern glue; coat the inside surfaces well, and cover and clamp as before, wiping up the excess that squeezes out. Use a casein glue; since it is water-soluble, there's a fair chance that it will bond to any bits of the old glue that remain behind.

If you want to be on the safe side, work a tiny file, a strip of sandpaper looped around a thin piece of wood, or any other flat abrasive tool under the flap. A disposable emery board will sometimes serve quite well. No matter what tool you use, remove all of the old glue. As a practical matter, you won't be able to clean off the surface all the way back to the point where it begins to bond again without running the risk of snapping off the flap of veneer. Do as thorough a job as you can, and reglue the flap, using a casein adhesive. Then cover the surface and clamp it as before.

Black spots

At first glance, many black spots look as if black ink had been spilled on the surface. This is not so. Most of the time the trouble comes from a long, continuous siege of moisture such as might be caused by a flower-pot resting on the surface. Do not try to scrape away the damage; you would quite likely hack your way halfway through the wood. Instead, a simple chemical treatment will almost always do the trick.

Buy some oxalic acid. This comes in the form of white crystals that look much like sugar. Most paint stores sell it in small boxes. When preparing a solution, don't bother to measure out precise proportions. Instead, start with about a cup of hot water and begin adding the oxalic acid crystals. Stir as you go. At one point the water won't accept any more of the crystals; they just won't dissolve but will remain in the bottom of the cup. When you've reached this stage, stop. The solution is ready to use. In general, figure on adding about three tablespoons of oxalic acid to a cup of water to get a working solution.

Brush this solution onto the black marks. They will disappear like

Fig. 13. Oxalic acid will bleach out black spots.

magic. Then wipe the surface thoroughly with a damp cloth. Allow the wood to dry completely. If when the wood has dried you find that some traces of the black marks or stains still remain, merely repeat the procedure. You may have to rebuild the finish, layer by layer. Wax and polish afterward.

Dents

Once again, dents look far more serious than they really are. There is a simple remedy that does work most of the time, but since it's not foolproof, a bit of luck helps too.

Merely place a small pad (slightly larger than the area of the dent itself) of rather moist (but not sopping-wet) cloth right over the dent. On top of this place a small disc of metal; a bottle cap or a coin will probably do. Apply the tip of a very hot iron to the metal disc. The cloth will get hot, and the steam will work down into the wood, where it will swell the fibers a bit. Stop briefly and check results. Stop when the dent is flush with the surface, or nearly so. Don't try for absolute perfection. There's always the danger that the steam may soften the finish. If you apply too

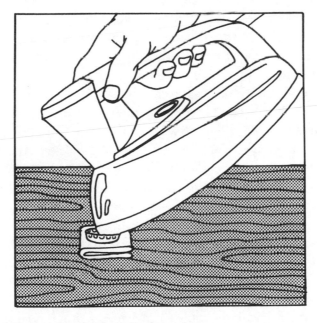

Fig. 14. Repairing a dent with an iron.

much heat or keep the iron in place too long, you'll have the added job of spot refinishing.

REPAIRING BEFORE REFINISHING

This type of repair includes work that is better done after the piece has been stripped of any previous finish. The work is easier on bare wood. But there's another reason: The action of the paint remover sometimes softens or dissolves some of the glue holding the furniture together. Frequently it pays to wait until all such damage is out of the way before starting the repair.

Loose rungs

Chair legs, table legs, and other furniture parts frequently get rickety with age. To tighten them up, start by removing all parts that are fastened together with nuts, bolts or screws. Then disassemble any glued joints that will come apart without extreme resistance. It's perfectly permissible to tap the sections apart with a soft-faced hammer, but don't clobber the wood to death.

If it is impossible to disassemble a joint, the piece of furniture was probably constructed with bulbous ends on the rungs. The old-time cabinetmakers frequently did this with chair construction. Because the only available glue was not very good, they frequently relied on the characteristics of the wood itself or on the forces of nature to hold their work together. For example, you may find that the legs and rungs of a chair are made of two different woods. This was intentional. The old-timers knew that wood would contract as it dried out. And they knew that if they forced the rungs into the legs, they would get extra pressure as the wood dried and the joint actually became more secure. Some of the better craftsmen added one more technique for additional insurance. They constructed the rungs so that the extreme ends were a little thicker. Then when the rungs were forced into the legs, the wood of the leg gripped this thicker section to make a joint that sometimes defies disassembly even today.

There's only one way to spot such a joint. Although it may be loose and rickety, it's almost impossible to take apart. Don't even try. Instead, use a glue injector to force new adhesive into the joint itself. This rela-

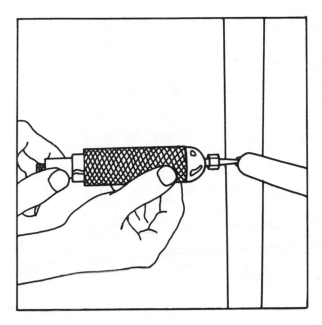

Fig. 15. Using a glue injector.

Fig. 16. Tightening a joint with cloth.

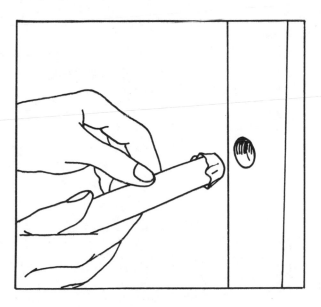

tively inexpensive tool looks like a large hypodermic needle and is available at most hardware stores. After drilling a small hole where the glue is to be inserted, place the tool in the hole and use it to direct the adhesive to the spot where it's needed. This maneuver can save a lot of harsh words.

For joints that can be taken apart, use this technique. Clean off the old glue from both surfaces—that is, the outside of the rung and the inside of the socket. Check the parts for play, and don't be surprised if they are wobbly. If this is the case, coat the socket and the rung tip with glue. Drape a small piece of soft cloth over the end of the rung, and then force the rung into the socket. The cloth will take up slack in the joint to make a reasonably tight connection. Trim off the excess cloth.

If the damage is beyond a simple repair like this, you may have to take more extreme measures. After cleaning out the socket thoroughly, glue a solid wood plug into the space and cut it off flush with the surface. When the adhesive has dried, drill out a new smaller-sized socket for the rung.

Put back the braces and other parts that are held in place with screws and bolts. If any of the screws will not tighten firmly, plug the hole with small sections of wood held in place with glue. Allow the adhesive to dry, and then drive the screw home into the reinforced surface.

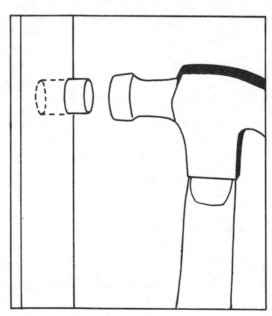

Fig. 17. Using a wood plug to repair a joint.

Cracks

This is a problem that often occurs with solid wood—the wood splits apart. However, quite frequently, when you take a close look at the damage, it's obvious that the so-called solid piece of wood is actually made up of several smaller sections. In any case, the result is the same. There's a structural defect that has to be corrected.

If possible, open up the crevice. You may be able to work in a wood wedge at one end or possibly force the parts open with your hands. Use only as much force as is necessary. Take a close look to see if it is indeed a solid piece of wood that has split, or whether it is made up of several smaller pieces. If it's one solid section, you can glue the parts back together without any further treatment. Use a good grade of casein glue for this, and work it down well into the crevice. If necessary, poke it down with a thin sliver of wood. It may help to tap the underside of the split with a rubber mallet. This tends to draw the glue down into place. Another maneuver is to rock the crack open and closed with your hands. Whichever technique you use, just make certain that the entire area of the break is completely coated with glue. Pad the surface with cloth;

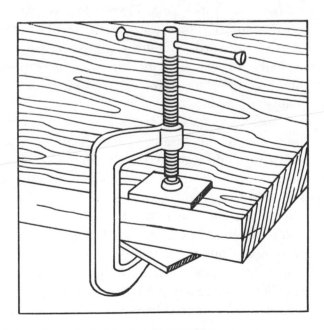

Fig. 18. Using a clamp to hold a crack together.

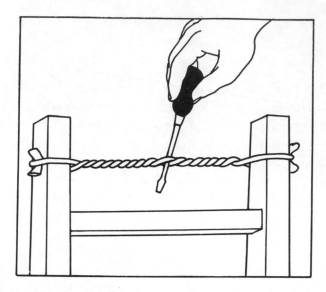

Fig. 19. The tourniquet method.

force the two halves together with a clamp, and keep the clamp in place until the glue has completely dried. After you've tightened the clamp, wipe off any excess glue that oozes out of the crevice with a damp cloth.

If you don't have furniture clamps in your tool kit, you can get by with a little improvisation. The tourniquet method will work quite well. Merely wrap strong, soft cord around the piece and tie the ends together, leaving plenty of slack. Slip a stick through the cord and twist it, tourniquet fashion. As with the clamps, be sure to pad the finished surfaces to avoid damaging them.

For smaller surfaces, a stack of books may provide enough pressure. Stout rubber bands (the type cut from old inner tubes) can be surprisingly effective; you'd be amazed at the amount of force you can generate by wrapping several of these bands tightly around a small joint.

There is one other home handyman's trick you should keep in mind in case you have to apply pressure to a flat surface. Let's say you're gluing down a large segment of veneer that has come loose from a tabletop. If you have disassembled the table so that you are working with just the top itself, there's an easy way to put pressure onto the surface after you have applied glue. Take the top down to the garage and put it on the cement floor. Add a layer of wax paper and a couple of sturdy boards on top. Then drive your car on the top so that one wheel rests on the boards. With this simple maneuver you can generate something on the order of half a ton of pressure. A magnitude such as this, however, should be used with extreme caution, and only if you have no other way to apply pressure.

Warped tabletops

There are two ways to attack a warped tabletop. The first, the path of the true craftsman, is arduous and tricky. This treatment involves cutting a series of saw kerfs partway through the wood, clamping the tabletop into a flat position, and filling the saw kerfs with thin strips of wood of matching type, color and grain. Then the surface has to be resanded and refinished. As you can see, this is not a one-evening project for the whole family.

However, if you are willing to substitute a bit of patience, it is still possible to straighten a bowed tabletop most of the time. Here's the process. Place the tabletop, bulge upward, on the ground. Pick a spot where the earth is flat and preferably covered with lawn grass. Place some weights on top of the bulge. Wait and hope. If you are in luck, the

Fig. 20. Repairing a warped tabletop.

moisture rising up from the ground will swell the wood on the underside. This will cause it to expand and will force the tabletop back to its original flat shape. The weights that you placed on top should help the process a bit. When the tabletop is flat again, dry the wood and seal it carefully with any protective finish so that moisture won't seep in again.

Loose drawer slides

If you take a close look at the drawer supports inside any chest, you'll discover a series of runners. Depending on the size of drawer and the type of construction, this might consist of two L-shaped slides at either side and, in larger or better-built pieces, a center support as well. In many cabinets, these are merely fastened to the sides with glue and a few small brads. The wear and tear of time plus the action of the paint remover can frequently loosen them.

The repair is simple. Merely scrape away any encrusted glue and fasten the slides in exactly the same position with more glue. Generally the wood will be darkened enough around the slides so as to outline their position. Add a few wire brads to hold the drawer slides in position until the adhesive has set. (You can then remove the brads, but you don't have to.) Fit the drawers back into place and check for proper fit. If necessary, adjust the slides.

Later, when you have refinished the piece, one of the final steps should be to rub the drawer slides and the matching sections of the drawer itself underneath with a stick-type lubricant that's made just for this job.

Loose joints

One of the disquieting aspects about stripping off old finish is that you are likely to find a whole batch of glue joints that seemed perfectly sturdy at first but are now quite loose. That's one of the not-quite-so-good side effects of removing finish. It doesn't always occur; it depends on the type of remover as well as the type of glue. But do be prepared for the possibility. If it should occur, just follow the procedures already detailed under Loose rungs (page 46) and Loose drawer slides (above).

Patching veneer

Gluing down a loose flap of veneer is a procedure that you can follow without damaging the finish of the furniture (see page 41). But if you want to replace a section of the veneer, this is an entirely different routine; and now, when the surface is completely bare, is the best time to tackle this job.

The process is surprisingly simple, if you are willing to follow the rules and use a bit of patience. Let's say there is a section of damaged veneer about the size of a half dollar right in the middle of an otherwise perfect tabletop. For the first step, find a piece of veneer to match that already in place on the surface. If you're in luck you may be able to pry a piece loose from some undersurface of the furniture. If not, buy some veneer that matches the original tone, wood and color as closely as possible.

Here's another surprise about patching veneer. A neat rectangular patch is probably the most obvious, and an irregularly shaped patch for some reason seems to blend in more thoroughly with the surface. So, for the first step, trim out an irregularly shaped piece of the new veneer large enough to cover the damage. Use a brand-new sharp razor blade and a straightedge for this job. Place the patch of veneer on top of the damaged area. Juggle it around a bit until the grain matches up as nearly as possible. Using the same razor blade, carefully mark a line all the way around the new patch. Work carefully and accurately.

Remove the patch and use the blade to cut through the outline of the patch on the old veneer. Some home handymen prefer to use an artist's or modelmaker's knife for this job. This tool comes with a series of different-shaped replaceable blades that fit into a pen-sized handle.

After cutting through the outline of the patch, pry up the veneer from the inside. A small chisel will generally work best. Be very careful not to gouge below the surface.

Using the razor blade or artist's knife, carefully scrape away any dried glue underneath. Make sure you are right down to the wood surface. Check the patch for perfect fit once more, and then apply new adhesive to the cut-out opening. Try to match the glue that was there, or use a casein glue. Place the patch in position and wipe up any excess glue. Cover the spot with a couple of layers of wax paper, and then apply

Fig. 21. Removing the damaged veneer.

pressure—using a clamp or weights—on top to force the patch firmly against the surface and keep it flat. Keep the clamps or weights in position until the glue has hardened.

When you take off the wax paper, you'll probably find that the patch is just slightly thicker than the surrounding area. This is perfectly fine. Use a razor blade to scrape off any excess adhesive that may have squeezed out above the surface. Then use a sanding block to sand the spot until the patch is perfectly level with the rest of the surface. If you've done a careful, craftsmanlike job, you'll be amazed at how invisible the repair work is, even close up.

Patches in solid wood

A very similar technique works quite well in patching serious mars in a solid wood surface. For example, let's say that the top of a chest of drawers has two square recesses cut in the place that formerly held a mirror in position, but since you don't intend to replace the mirror, the cutouts appear to be a minor disaster. Or let's say that a tabletop has such a deep burn or mar in it that there's no possibility of leveling the area with wood filler.

The repairs are not as complicated as they may seem. As with the veneer patch, start the job by locating a piece of wood that as nearly as possible resembles the original surface in grain, color and tone. Sometimes it is possible to take a piece from the back surface of a drawer, if it's made of the same wood as the top. There may be a section of trim that can be sacrificed. If not, do the best you can by using a piece of new wood. Calculate the thickness of the patch or plug that will be required. Don't figure on using a piece of wood that's thinner than a quarter of an inch.

Cut out the patch or plug first. As with veneer, an irregular shape will tend to hide the repair a bit better than a nice square patch. After you have cut out the patch, place it on top of the surface, covering the mar. Once again, draw around it with a sharp razor blade or the point of a scribe. Be as accurate as possible.

Using a sharp wood chisel, cut a groove all the way around the marked patch. Then very carefully remove the wood inside the mark.

Try to remove the wood evenly, although it's not necessary to work to micrometer precision. Keep testing with the patch, and plan to work in layers, marking off the outline and then removing the wood inside. The patch should be thick, but it does not have to be as deep as the mar. When you have cut an opening deep enough so that the patch is almost but not quite flush, you are ready for the next stage.

Apply glue to the recess and to the underside of the patch. Use animal glue if the furniture is old, casein glue if it is new. Fit the patch into position, and if necessary force it down into place. A little man-handling is perfectly permissible here.

Use weights or clamps to hold the patch in place until the glue is hardened. Then level the patch until it is flush with the surface. If you have to remove much material, start with a plane. Work carefully, one stroke at a time. When you are almost flush with the surface, check to make certain the plug fits smoothly without any crevices between new and old wood. If there are any openings, no matter how minute, this is the time to fill them in. Use wood filler and work it into place with a putty knife.

When the filler has dried, use a sanding block to sand the spot, working along the grain of the wood until the patch is perfectly level with the surface.

This is a good time to check over the furniture for any other minor repairs that need to be made. For example, loose drawer pulls are fixed by tightening the screws inside the drawer. Sometimes knobs are held in place with dowels; work them loose, clean off the old encrusted glue, and apply new adhesive.

Bits of trim (assuming they've been saved) are not difficult to glue back into place. Just make sure the meeting surfaces are clean and dry. If necessary, add a few small brads to hold the sections in position until the glue dries. If the wood is very thin or appears to be brittle, it's a good idea to drill pilot holes before driving in any brads, to avoid splitting the wood. This is also a fine time to replace casters, broken hinges, and other bits of hardware.

REMOVING THE OLD FINISH 4

MANY PEOPLE FEEL that furniture finishing—coloring, toning, coating wood—gives them a sense of artistry. However, when it comes to stripping the finish off furniture, you can forget this idea. It's messy all the way. The good part is that you may well emerge with a real sense of satisfaction. This is the first time you see the potential in a piece of furniture. Up until now it has probably been coated with an assortment of paint, varnish and lacquer, plus the grime of years. After stripping it you will get a good indication of just how attractive the finished piece can be.

Working conditions are important when stripping finish off furniture. Your best bet is to work outdoors. A shady spot under a tree would be the ideal work area. However, do realize that the various chemicals used in removing paint are highly corrosive. For this reason, if you dribble them liberally on the ground, you may be instituting your own "scorched earth" policy. It may be some time before greenery comes up in that immediate area again.

Surprisingly enough, you will be using a great deal of water in finishing furniture. The surface has to be washed down thoroughly, and the easiest way to do this job is with a garden hose. That's why the outdoors is so ideal.

Second best is an open porch with a roof over it for shade. This will give you plenty of ventilation so the fumes from the chemicals don't have a chance to become concentrated.

If you do have to work indoors, a basement area is the most likely place. It should have a drain in the floor so that the furniture can be washed down thoroughly at several points along the way. Make sure there is sufficient ventilation. Ideally there should be a window at either end of the work area; you can open them and have a fan blowing out through one window. This will pull fresh air through the other window, with the breeze going right across your work area. This ventilation is very important. Even if you can't smell them, the fumes from some paint-removing chemicals may be irritating and should be avoided.

Dress carefully for the job. Wear a long-sleeved shirt, a hat, and a pair of heavy-duty gloves; the kind that are fabric-lined and thicker than normal household gloves are a worthwhile investment. Some people get allergic reactions to the chemicals used in paint removers. There is no need to find out the hard way just how sensitive your skin is; merely avoid all contact with the stuff. Buy a pair of goggles and wear them whenever you work with paint remover. It's so easy to get a little careless, and all it takes is one drop of the remover spattered in your eye to cause extreme discomfort.

As a final safety precaution, don't smoke while you are working. Many of the chemicals are nonflammable, but others can be highly combustible. It's easier to make a blanket no-smoking rule than to keep tabs on what type of solution you are using.

PAINT REMOVER

Main types of paint remover

1. Liquid: As the name indicates, this comes in the form of a free-flowing liquid.
2. Paste: It's not really a paste; it's more like a thick cream. However, because it has more body, it's easier to use on vertical surfaces because it will not drip or sag as readily.

In between these primary types are lots of different varieties, but you can become an instant expert merely by reading the labels carefully and following instructions exactly.

Which brand of paint remover?

There's no real answer to this question, because no one brand of paint remover will work in all situations. And there's no accurate way to predict which remover will work on a particular surface. For this reason your best bet is to test a spot before starting work on the entire piece of furniture. At the paint or hardware store, buy the smallest containers of several different brands and types of paint remover. Try them out one at a time. In short order you'll be able to tell which one best handles the particular finish you want to remove.

One more general rule about commercial paint removers: Read the label carefully. It's amazing just how much useful information you will find on it. For example, some types of paint remover require a neutralizer to prepare the wood for finishing; some claim that no cleanup or washup is necessary after they have been used. Others contain wax to keep the solvent in the chemical from evaporating too rapidly. Some of this wax is left behind after the surface has been cleaned off and has to be removed with a special wash so the new finish can adhere. If you are working in the backyard, the "wash-away" type removers are handy. Instead of scraping off the softened finish, you can frequently blast it off with the garden hose. As you can see, this is definitely an outdoor project.

If you intend to do a great deal of furniture stripping, you might also experiment with some of the paint removers sold (in large quantities) through auto supply stores. These are used by the companies that refinish auto bodies. Quite often the same chemicals are highly effective on wood finishes. Here again, it's a matter of testing. Buy a small container of the material and try it out. If it does the job with no side reactions, you have the possibility of saving yourself a happy bit of change.

Other tools and materials

Buy a couple of sleeves of steel wool in the grades known as 4/0 and 3/0 (incidentally, that's pronounced four-oh and three-oh). You also need a flexible-blade putty knife. Check the edge carefully to make certain it's not too sharp, or you will tend to dig the blade into the wood. If the metal is sharp, use a file to round the edges slightly. At the same time, check the corners of the blade. If necessary round them with the file too.

Working procedure

To get ready, put down a tarpaulin if you are working indoors, or if you are concerned for the greenery outdoors. The old-type canvas ones are best; they are heavy and are much more expensive than the plastic kind, but they'll stand a great deal more abuse. If you do opt for a plastic one, spend a few cents more and get the thicker plastic film. Those super-thin plastic sheets that masquerade as tarpaulins have virtually no durability at all. Whatever kind of tarpaulin you use, put down a layer of three or four sheets of newspaper over the entire surface. Newspaper absorbs a great deal of moisture, prolongs the life of the tarpaulin, and simplifies the clean-up process.

Plan to work on one piece of furniture at a time, especially when tackling your first furniture-finishing project. You see, you're learning, and it's easier on a small-scale basis: one section at a time, one drawer at a time.

Plan the work area so that you do most of the job at waist height. Otherwise you're likely to get a sore back. This means that you may need some raised work surfaces such as sawhorses. Just make certain they're sturdy and will support the furniture firmly. Raise chests and tables on small wooden blocks. Thread spools are ideal for this job. Merely tack them in place on the undersides of the legs. The idea is to lift the furniture so it doesn't sit in the puddles of paint remover that form.

Collect a batch of clean cans to hold the paint remover and other chemicals. It's a shame that coffee cans have been restyled in recent years. The older type that was shallower but larger in diameter was especially handy for this job. However, the contemporary kind does almost as well.

As applicators, select brushes in the 1- to 3-inch-wide range. You don't want good brushes for this job, but the bristles should be natural; some synthetics actually dissolve in paint remover. A stubby brush is more useful than one with long, flowing bristles.

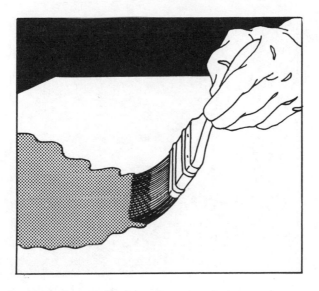

Fig. 22. Flowing the remover on.

There is as much of an art to applying paint remover as there is to painting, but it's simple to learn. Merely flow the remover on, or, as the painters say, lay it on the surface. Do not brush. The object is to saturate the area rather than to exercise your artistry. Dip the brush frequently and use a series of short strokes. If the remover flows down toward one corner, block up the piece of furniture until it is level. If possible, do one surface at a time, and turn the piece as you go, so that the working side is always on top and always level. If this isn't practical, you can apply paint remover to a vertical surface; this is a little easier if you use the heavier paste type. Apply it in a series of horizontal bands, starting at the top of the surface.

Then wait. This is probably the most critical step in the entire process. It's so easy to become impatient, which just makes the job take more time. It's important to let the chemicals do all the work.

Every now and then test the surface with the brush. The object is to remove all of the old finish at one time, right down to the bare wood. If you tackle the work one layer at a time, the job can take forever. If the finish isn't softening beyond the first layer or so, simply add more paint remover right on top. Just slap it on. Keep adding layers as long as the finish will accept it. Always allow the full waiting time suggested on the remover's label in between coats for the chemicals to work.

Fig. 23. Scraping the remover and the old finish off.

At one point as you are slapping on what seems to be the umpteenth layer of remover, the brush will cut through to the bare wood below. Allow a little more waiting time, and then see if the entire finish will slide off when you gently scrape with the putty knife. If a layer or so still adheres to the surface, add more remover and rustle up some more patience.

If the putty knife does reveal the bare wood, keep moving it in a strip all the way across from one end of the surface to the other. Be sure to work with the grain of the wood to minimize any possibility of creating scratches. Hold a coffee can or similar container under the far edge; to catch the softened paint as you work you'll also have a handy surface on which to scrape off the blade of the putty knife. When you have done one strip, go back and do the next. You should be able to remove the entire finish in a series of parallel strips.

If all of the finish does not come loose and reveal the bare wood underneath—*stop*. Apply more remover and wait. If you try to scrape it off before the entire layer is softened, you're just making more work for yourself.

One indication that the paint remover is acting is that the softened surface will wrinkle. The paint will pull together in a set of gummy lines. When the same wrinkled condition extends all the way through the layers of accumulated coatings, leaving the bare wood exposed underneath, the remover is fully effective.

To get off the last bit of the finish, rub the surface with a pad of steelwool that has been dipped in the paint remover.

Neutralizing

To neutralize the remover, wash down the surface well with lacquer thinner or alcohol. This is very important. If you have used one of the heavier type removers or one of the varieties that contain wax, do not skimp on the alcohol wash. As a matter of fact, repeat the process two or three times, or else you will wind up with spots on the surface where the new finish simply will not adhere.

Water cleanup

Some removers are designed to be flushed away. Certainly this process is handy and easy. Instead of scraping off the softened finish, you merely turn a hose onto the piece of furniture and blast away at it. This definitely must be done outdoors or in a basement with a floor drain. Do not try to get by with buckets of water or cloths—they simply won't work. You'll wind up with a fantastic mess. It's the hose or nothing.

Fig. 24. Cleaning up with a hose.

Difficult surfaces

Clean the softened finish from moldings and trim with a small, stiff, short-bristled brush soaked in paint remover. For curves, use a pad of steel wool soaked in paint remover. Turned surfaces such as chair legs can be cleaned with a strip of burlap dipped in paint remover; hold one end in each hand and use the shoeshine technique. All hardware should be removed from the furniture and cleaned separately. Soak it in a can of paint remover until all the finish can be brushed off with a wire brush.

Place wide-mouth tin cans under the legs of furniture so that as you work down the vertical surfaces, the remover will flow from the furniture into the tin cans. Otherwise it's quite likely to spread all over the floor. If you're working on a piece of furniture where both the top surface and underside have to be stripped (such as a tabletop), do the underside first. Clean it off completely and then flip the piece over. Support it on blocks so that it is raised from the work surface, and treat the top surface.

Drawers are always removed from a chest for paint removing. Since you will probably be working on these with the front surface facing up, it's a good idea to plug any holes left when you removed the hardware; use a strip of paper towel rolled into a taper shape. Then the paint remover will not run inside the drawer.

LYE

Lye has been cursed and praised in almost every language and accent around the world. As a last-ditch process, it can perform prodigious feats in removing tough, obstinate finishes. It's also fast and cheap. However, it is extremely caustic. If you get any of it on your skin, it may leave a serious burn. Also, the fumes are no joy to inhale.

Lye can only be used in warm weather—when the temperature is 70° F. or more. In addition, you'll definitely need an available hose, since the cleanup involves large amounts of water.

You can buy lye in crystals in most hardware and paint stores. It's usually sold as a drain cleaner. Buy the cheapest kind you can find; lye is lye, and there's no need to get fancy. You'll also need a metal bucket and a pair of extra-heavy rubber gloves with a long cuff that extends up your arm. Dress for the occasion: a long-sleeved shirt, a hat, and most important of all, well-fitting protective goggles. The danger accelerates if the lye gets anywhere near your eyes. For the applicator, make a mop from a wooden stick with several layers of cloth wired in position at the end. For smaller jobs you can get by with an old-fashioned string dish mop.

Mix the solution in the metal bucket by adding one standard-size can of lye to one quart of water. Always add the lye to the water. If you try it the other way around, the solution may boil up out of the container.

Using lye

Flow the solution onto the piece of furniture; mop it until the finish dissolves. If there are any crevices, push the lye into them with a scraper or wire brush. As with regular paint remover, the materials should be softened right down to the bare wood.

When one entire surface is soft, wash it off with a hose set for the hardest possible stream. It's absolutely necessary to use lots of water. Use a scrub brush (the old-fashioned kind used on the kitchen floor) to

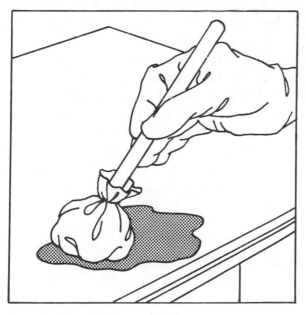

Fig. 25. Applying lye with a mop.

remove the last traces of lye. Keep the hose going as you scrub. This step is very critical. Any lye remaining in the wood may actually burn or rot it, or at least cause some bad discoloration.

Neutralize the lye

After treating the entire piece of furniture, wipe the surface as dry as possible. The best neutralizing agent is plain ordinary vinegar. Buy the cheapest kind in the largest container you can find in your grocery store. Swab this all over the surface of the wood, and be careful that you don't skip any areas. Rinse the surface a second time with more water, using either the hose or thick wet cloths. Dry the piece off once more. The wood will take several days indoors at normal temperatures to dry out completely, so don't plan to proceed with the finishing right away.

Patch-up bleach

One of the unfortunate characteristics of lye is that it darkens the wood. This may be perfectly fine if you are going to apply an antique finish, because with a clear finish on top it does give a nice soft patina or glow of age to the wood. However, if you want to re-create the original surface, you'll have to lighten the darkened effect.

If this is the case, use ordinary household bleach instead of vinegar for neutralizing. Swab it on and make sure you cover all sections. Keep an eye on the color of the wood. When it seems to have lightened to the shade you are seeking, wash the furniture with lots of water and dry it.

If you have used a great deal of lye or if you have left it on for quite a long time, the bleach may not be strong enough to lighten the wood. In this case use oxalic acid (see page 84). Swab it onto the furniture in exactly the same way as you used the bleach. Wash it off thoroughly and then dry the furniture.

REMOVING BUTTERMILK PAINT

There comes a time in the life of every home craftsman when instant frustration sets in. You have been having fantastically good luck stripping away the layers of finish. It all came off rather easily. However, underneath everything is a final layer of reddish-brown pigment that simply refuses to budge. None of the removers even makes a dent.

You have probably hit a layer of "buttermilk paint." This was an old favorite among colonial cabinetmakers and homeowners. They mixed pigment and other ingredients with some buttermilk that was not good enough to sell and thereby fashioned a homemade paint. Think twice before you remove it. Such a coating is generally the sign of a genuine antique. Unless you are determined to have a natural wood finish, you may destroy a considerable amount of value simply by getting rid of this kind of paint. Museums have many classic pieces of furniture that are finished with it.

If you do want to strip away this antique paint, however, there is a material that will cut through it: ordinary household ammonia. Use it straight, as it comes from the bottle, mopping it in place with a thick pad of very fine steel wool. Keep buffing with the steel wool as you work until the paint is completely dissolved. Rinse the piece with water to neutralize the ammonia, and then dry it thoroughly.

As with several other removers, this one tends to darken the wood. If you find this objectionable, use the bleach and rinse-water technique described on page 66.

TRISODIUM PHOSPHATE

In those good old days when household products seemed to work a lot better, many cleaners for floors and walls contained healthy amounts of trisodium phosphate. Now it's a minor ingredient at best. It is a highly effective and rather inexpensive paint remover. You can buy it in the form of a dry powder in most large paint and hardware stores. Dissolve as much of the material as possible in a quantity of hot water. Generally you can add from 2½ to 3½ cups of trisodium phosphate to a gallon of water. This may vary according to the water temperature; the hotter the water, the more material will dissolve. Keep adding the chemical until no more will dissolve.

Use the material hot. If necessary keep a container of it on a hotplate so that it will remain just under boiling. Use a mop to apply it, and finish up with steel wool pads. Scrub as you go, and if necessary remove the finish one layer at a time. As with lye and some of the other caustic removers, this material may darken the surface of the wood. If so, use the bleach treatment.

There are several advantages to this material. For one thing it's not nearly so caustic as lye. And professional strippers use it in their dip tanks because it is rather inexpensive yet effective.

REMOVING PLASTIC COATINGS

It is a foregone conclusion that every home craftsman will eventually come upon a piece of furniture that has been finished with one of the new plastic coatings (such as polyurethane). Some of these have truly wonderful qualities, but if you're trying to strip them off wood, the experience can be frustrating. There are some coatings that shrug off the entire range of ordinary paint-removing chemicals.

Since the exotic-type removers are not readily available to home craftsmen, there are only two practical courses of action open. You can start scraping. Just resign yourself to the fact that it's going to be a long, tedious process. You actually have to remove a microscopic layer of the wood. Ease the job with disposable-blade scrapers, and try to keep the bad language to a minimum.

Or see if you can find a company that does sandblasting. Such firms may be listed in the Yellow Pages under "Stone Cutters." They specialize in handling the lettering on buildings and tombstones; and, surprisingly, the same technique can clean almost everything off the surface of furniture. What's left behind is a fairly rough surface, but sanding is still easier than scraping.

SMOOTHING THE SURFACE 5

THIS ASPECT OF the work carries with it a real sense of craftsmanship. It's not messy (except for a bit of sawdust), it's not really difficult, and there are no annoying fumes to disturb your tranquillity. And it's at this stage that the true beauty of the wood will begin to emerge beneath your hands.

There is a definite art and technique to smoothing wood. Happily, the easy way is the best way. The process involves three fundamental ideas:

1. All abrasives cause scratches. Even the very finest grades—those with surfaces so smooth that they resemble sheets of fine writing paper—will cause scratches. You may have to find them with a microscope, but they're there. However, that's the secret of smoothing wood. Each finer grade of abrasive that you use removes the scratches caused by the previous grade. At the end you have worked your way down to a wood surface that feels as smooth as glass.

2. The smoothing process involves a balancing. The coarser grades of abrasive may appear to work faster (at least they produce more sawdust), but you'll need more steps with successively finer grades to complete the job. On the other hand, fine abrasives work so slowly that the process will seem to take forever. It's best to use the coarser grades to

remove surface mars and abrasions. Then, as quickly as possible, move on to finer grades to complete the job.

3. Never sand across the grain; always work in the direction of the grain. The lines of the wood will tend to conceal scratches and be more forgiving. Cross-grain scratches are difficult to remove and very evident.

ABRASIVE PAPER

Sandpaper, that old reliable material, actually comes in a whole host of types, varieties, and components. You'll do a better job if you select the precise abrasive for the task. Here are the various factors you should consider.

Type of grit

1. Flint: This is what everybody means by the term sandpaper. It's the cheapest, most common kind, but it doesn't last very long. It is a wise choice if you're working on a surface that will clog the grit. For example, you may be removing the last bits of in-grained paint from a tabletop. Since the coating will clog the pores of the abrasive paper, a better quality of abrasive would just be wasted. Save your money—use flint.

2. Garnet: This material has a satisfying blend of characteristics. Many cabinetmakers like it because the abrasive granules are hard enough to cut through the wood surface with satisfying results. At the same time, the granules tend to fracture or break off. This exposes a new series of cutting edges, so the abrasive usually lasts considerably longer and remains effective longer, too.

3. Aluminum oxide: This material starts to get into the heavy-duty area of abrasives. The particles are considerably more rugged and are well anchored in place. The sheet has a speckled gray-black appearance. Because the surface has an extra-long life, this is a favorite for use in power sanders, but it is equally well suited for handwork.

4. Silicon carbide: Like aluminum oxide, this is a man-made abrasive material, and quite an effective one, too. It's a uniform black color, with a very even layer of cutting particles. Equally

suitable for use on metal or wood, it's more frequently used in the finer grades.

Size of particles

There are several grading systems to cover the range of coarse to fine abrasive, but you'll avoid confusion and use the right grade of sandpaper if you understand two classification methods. The first is a number arrangement that runs from a rough abrasive known as No. 80 to a fine surface designated No. 600. The other method utilizes the "0" system. The abrasive corresponding to No. 80 is 1/0 (pronounced "one-oh"). The one corresponding to No. 600 is 12/0.

As a practical matter you will almost never need this entire range. Most of your work will be confined to three—or at the most four—grades of sandpaper. The rest of the assortment is there for the odd, occasional task that requires some specialized abrasive. The following chart tells you which grade to use.

GRADES OF SANDPAPER

80 or 1/0	Use for rough work when a considerable amount of material has to be removed and for shaping surfaces.
100 or 2/0	
120 or 3/0	Use this as the first step in preparing a piece of furniture that has just been stripped of an old finish. It is satisfactory for removing most scratches and surface mars, as long as they are not too deep.
150 or 4/0	
180 or 5/0	Use this grade as the workhorse of your project. It will make the most significant difference in the transition from a rough surface to a smooth one.
220 or 6/0	
240 or 7/0	Most craftsmen consider this the final grade for smoothing a surface before painting. On soft woods, finer grades will just clog immediately.
280 or 8/0	
320 or 9/0	Use for the final sanding on hard, dense woods, such as walnut and mahogany. It is also useful for sanding between coats or after bleach, or for dulling the surface of hard high-gloss finishes.
400 or 10/0	
500 or 11/0	Use to scuff the surface of fully dry and hard-gloss finishes to create a dull sheen or eggshell effect. It can be used wet on some finishes.
600 or 12/0	

Open or closed grit

Abrasive paper can be manufactured with the particles of grit spaced closely together or relatively far apart. "Closed" grits have particles clumped closely together. Because there are more cutting edges to do the work, they will smooth the surface in less time. However, they also tend to clog up with sawdust, old finish, or anything else. There's no place for this debris to go.

"Open" grits, with space around the particles, will last far longer. However, it will take longer to achieve the same degree of smoothness. You will have to decide which to use for each job, once you get a feel of the way the work is going. If clogging is a problem, switch to an open grit. If the work seems to be taking forever, try a closed grit, and see if it will smooth the surface without too much clogging.

Wet or dry

Some abrasive papers are waterproof and can be used with water as a lubricant. Of course this is completely impractical on bare wood surfaces. However, for smoothing really hard finishes, such as polyurethane or the harder varnishes, or for working on metal, the wet-type paper is useful. This does not mean that you must use it wet; it just indicates that the option is available to you.

Dry papers do not have a waterproof backing or adhesive to hold the grit in place. For this reason they must be used dry. In general, abrasive papers that can be used wet are more expensive; it's a needless waste to buy such a sheet when the work is to be sanded dry.

There is also an adaptable material called wet-or-dry which can be used under either condition.

How to Use Sandpaper

If the finished piece is to be painted, you merely have to sand the surface completely smooth, after filling dents and scratches with wood filler. You do not have to treat dark stains and other small mars that don't affect the smoothness of the surface, since you're going to cover them with an opaque finish.

Most enamel finishes today are self-leveling; that is, before they dry, they adjust to form a smooth surface, eliminating brush marks and the like. As a by-product of this, and also because paint is a relatively thick coating, you do not have to be quite so careful in sanding the undersurface. If you use 5/0 abrasive paper for the final smoothing process, you'll get excellent results. More work will rarely pay off in terms of a superior final effect, so save your muscle.

Transparent or translucent finishes are a different story entirely. If the grain of the wood is to show, the surface must be noticeably smoother than for painted surfaces. To achieve this, you'll have to follow the complete smoothing routine, finishing with 7/0 paper for the final stage for soft woods, or 8/0 or 9/0 for dense cabinet woods.

Sanding block

A simple sanding block makes a noticeable difference in the finished job as well as in the work itself. It's nothing more than a one-inch-thick scrap of wood cut to a size that you can wrap a quarter-sheet

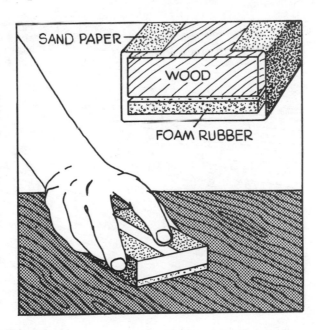

Fig. 26. Sanding block.

of sandpaper around. A block of this dimension is generally conveniently palm-sized, so you can work without fatigue.

One other feature is quite necessary. Glue a thin layer (about one-quarter inch thick) of foam rubber or felt to the working surface of the block. The sandpaper wraps around the padded surface. There is more than comfort involved, because there's less tendency for the sandpaper to gouge the surface, and less heat and less clogging. Just that thin flexible layer will allow the abrasive sheet to adjust to minor variations in the surface.

Many hardware and paint stores sell commercially made sanding blocks. Some of them contain rolls of sandpaper that you pull out from inside each time a new surface is needed. Spend the money if you want to; the home variety will work just as well.

Sanding technique

Use firm, even pressure. Do not bear down; let the abrasive do all the work. Rub in straight lines following the grain of the wood; never go across the grain. This back-and-forth technique takes a bit of practice,

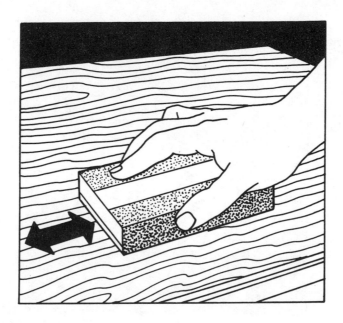

Fig. 27. Sand with the grain, never across it.

because it's difficult to maintain discipline on such a routine, picky job. But it is necessary, since cross-grain scratches are difficult to remove.

Theoretically, when you work down to the very fine grades of abrasive paper, you can sand in any direction you want. Do not believe this! All it takes is one outsized particle of grit on the sheet of abrasive paper to put you back about three steps in your sanding schedule.

Sanding schedule

Make sure the surface is flat and level, and at a convenient working height. There's nothing worse for the worker than an awkward bent-over position. If you are comfortable, the work will go more quickly and easily.

Select the proper grade paper and type of abrasive. Tear the sheet into quarters and wrap one section around the sanding block.

Begin at one corner of the surface and work evenly back and forth. Do not concentrate on any one single section unless it has some repairs or mars that have to be worked down. Try to make your sanding as even as possible.

As each grade of abrasive completes the work it was designed to do, switch to the next finer grade. The change-over time is relatively easy to determine. When there are no longer any scratches on the surface deeper than those produced by the abrasive you're using, it's time to switch. If you have trouble spotting this, check the work in cross-light. This will emphasize the scratches. Now (before the finish goes on) is the only time you can effectively remove them. Certain types of finishes actually seem to amplify unnoticed scratches, and that can be enough to break the craftsman's heart.

Moisten the surface of the wood with a damp but not wet sponge. The idea is to slightly wet the fibers of the wood that are right at the surface. Coat the entire sanded area as evenly as possible. This technique will swell and raise the tiny fibers of wood that have been pressed down by sanding. Allow the surface to dry overnight, and then give it one final sanding with the finest grade of abrasive paper you have used.

Final touch

There's one old-time cabinetmaker's technique that you may want to use occasionally for special effects. It's called burnishing, and there are two ways to do it. Let's say you've made a repair to the furniture—used filler, glued some sections together, et cetera. There's a chance that this new area may accept the finish in a different manner from the rest of the piece. However, burnishing can help equalize the effect. For a small area, cut a small block of hardwood such as maple or birch and sand it until it is very, very smooth. Using lots of pressure, rub this briskly over the spot. It will heat the wood slightly and, in effect, iron down the wood fibers so they are slightly compressed.

There is a similar technique that can be used on the entire tabletop. Cover a block of wood with raw, untanned, untreated leather. Again, using lots of pressure, rub this briskly over the surface. It acts in pretty much the same manner. You will glaze and compress the tiny fibers of wood on the surface. The resulting texture is like plate glass. This is definitely not a technique for everyday use but handy to know for that special finishing job.

Assorted hints and tips

There are several small tricks that you can utilize in smoothing wood to make the job go more swiftly or to save effort.

For smoothing surfaces such as turned chair legs, cut the abrasive paper into strips, and back each one with a strip of transparent tape to add some strength. Use this in a back-and-forth shoeshine technique all the way around and up and down the chair leg.

Be careful when you are sanding a veneered surface. There's no way to tell how much of the material has already been removed or how thin the remaining layer is. The best technique is to remove as little of the veneer as possible. Keep an eye on the surface as you work for signs of sanding through.

When sanding the sides of drawers, always work back and forth in the direction they slide. Also, after you have smoothed it, seal the wood with spray lacquer. This will keep the drawers operating smoothly.

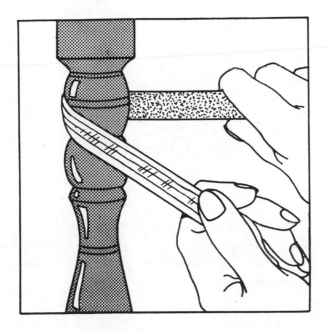

Fig. 28. The shoeshine technique for sanding chair legs.

Before you use any new piece of abrasive paper, always scuff it, grit to grit, against another piece of the same paper; this will help to knock off any outsized particles of the abrasive that can spoil the surface.

Don't be too quick to throw out used abrasive paper unless it is so completely loaded with old finish that it's totally useless. Even though it may look worn out, used abrasive paper can be useful. It may be slow in cutting action, but the abrasive surface is perfectly even, so it won't produce any unexpected scratches. Many professional cabinetmakers consider this a bonus and save used paper for the final rubdown before going on to the next finer grade.

POWER SANDERS

These handy muscle-saving tools come in several varieties. Select very carefully, however. Some types are totally unsuitable for furniture finishing.

Straight-line or back-and-forth sander

As the name indicates, this sander grips a large sheet of sandpaper and moves it back and forth. Such a tool is usable for all pieces of work, starting with the first rough sanding all the way up to the final gloss. Because it cuts in only one direction, it will not make cross-grain scratches.

Better quality straight-line sanders are powered by a regular motor and are fairly large. They also come in a junior-sized version that's powered by a vibrator motor. You can easily spot this tool because it makes a noise like a gigantic angry mosquito. In general, vibrator sanders, although they may have the right action, don't have enough power for anything but small-scale jobs.

Belt sander

This workhorse uses an endless belt of sandpaper that rotates around two rollers. As a result, there's considerable abrasive action available when using this sander. Since the action is in only one direction, there's no possibility of cross-grain scratches, unless you get careless in directing the tool. It can be used for all steps in the sanding process.

A few precautions might be in order, however. For one thing, because this sander probably has the fastest cutting action of any on the market, it's very easy to sand right through thin veneer or to actually make uneven spots in the wood. For this reason, keep it moving constantly and make sure that the action is always directed with the grain of the wood. These units all require special belts of sandpaper, but these are generally available in a variety of types and grits.

Orbital sander

The action here is in a circular plane, although the sander itself does not spin. If you have any doubt about whether a sander is straight-line or orbital, just turn it upside down so that the sandpaper pad faces up. Make a pencil dot on it, and turn on the power. The straight-line sander will transform the dot into a line, while an orbital sander will create a circle.

An orbital sander can be used for the first or rough phase of the job, but beyond this it tends to create more problems than it solves. Because the cutting action is in all directions, it makes scratches cross-grain. As has been repeatedly emphasized, this is not good.

Not suitable

There are two types of sanders that are relatively common but should not be used for furniture finishing. The first is the disc sander. It is the cheapest abrasive power unit on the market, and most of the time it comes in the form of a rubber disc designed to hook into the chuck of a quarter-inch electric drill. Discs of sandpaper are attached to the underside of the rubber disc. This tool is probably suitable for removing paint or for other rough abrasive jobs, but it is not good for fine work. It creates swirl marks in the surface and is also rather hard to control because it tends to skitter out of position.

In the same category is the drum sander. This tool consists of a metal cylinder with the sandpaper attached to the outside surface. Because the cutting action is concentrated, this device tends to sand ruts into the surface of the wood. It's almost impossible to get a smooth surface with a hand-held drum sander. There are large standing units that have precision controls. The wood is led into them rather like lumber on a saw table. Although they do an excellent job, this kind of power equipment is well beyond the province of even an advanced craftsman.

Be sure to read the instructions that come with whichever type of power sander you decide to purchase. If the sander is to function properly, the abrasive paper must be inserted and secured according to the instructions. Use the same grade of sandpaper for power sanders as you would for handwork. Always practice on some scrap wood before tackling furniture. Although not difficult to use, all these tools do require a bit of practice as part of the learning process.

BLEACHING 6

BLEACH IS A powerful material. It stands to reason that anything strong enough to take the coloring out of wood fibers can hardly be classed as a weak substance. This does not mean it's dangerous, at least not if you exercise common sense. In short, bleach is a useful material that will perform a valuable function in finishing furniture. Use it carefully and wisely.

HOW TO USE BLEACH

Work area

Ventilation is essential. Some of the bleaching chemicals can irritate your eyes or lungs if you're exposed to them for long periods of time. Even the milder chemicals such as laundry bleach can have the same effect. After all, this is not the same process as dumping some of it into the washing machine. You are spreading the material over quite an extensive surface, so there's a lot of it to evaporate and irritate.

The ideal working area is out-of-doors. Again, if you can work in the shade (under a big tree, under a covered porch), you will have the fewest problems with the chemicals.

Be sure to put down a dropcloth with several layers of newspaper on top. While this process is not nearly so messy as paint removing, it's hardly a dining table procedure.

Safety precautions

Wear rubber gloves. The heavy-duty ones with long cuffs are well worth the slight additional investment. Household-type rubber gloves will do, but they don't hold up very well. As for those transparent plastic gloves, forget them. The thin film used to make them tears very quickly.

If you get any bleach on your skin, wash it off immediately with lots of clear water. If you don't have running water close at hand, be sure to have a bucket of it beside you for just this purpose. Wear long-sleeved clothing and a hat to protect your skin. Also, inexpensive goggles are essential to protect your eyes from spatters.

There's one other precaution, and it may be an unexpected one. Almost any bleach you use will raise the grain of the wood. This means you will have to resand the surface with very fine abrasive paper after it is dry. Keep in mind that the surface of the wood still has some of the chemical residue in it, and it will float through the air as you sand. This is especially true if you are using a power sander. So that you don't inhale the dust and chemicals, buy and wear an inexpensive painter's mask that covers your nose and mouth. These masks contain several cloth pads that are quite adequate for filtering out the noxious dust.

Preparations

It's important to spend enough time on advance preparations if you want the bleach to act smoothly and evenly. The wood surface must be completely free of grease, wax, and all traces of old finish. In addition, the wood should be sanded smooth.

Testing

The results of bleaching chemicals are not always predictable. There is absolutely no guarantee that the results will be the same each time you use the material. After all, you are applying it to a natural material, and wood is anything but predictable.

For this reason, always test first. If possible, apply the bleach to a scrap of the same wood. This will at least give you some clue as to the results you may expect. If this isn't practical, use a hidden part of the wood, such as the underside of a chair seat or drawer.

Applicators

Do not use your good brushes for this job. As a matter of fact, natural bristles may be damaged by the chemicals. To apply bleach, use inexpensive synthetic fiber brushes. If you prefer, a wad of clean white cloth will do just as well. You can wire it onto a stick to make a swab, or tackle the job by hand (wearing rubber gloves, of course).

Even application

Even though the surface may look perfectly smooth and regular, there's a possibility that the bleach may take irregularly. To get around this problem, you have to help the bleaching action along. The process is simple. Using a handful of steel wool or a nylon mesh pot scourer, scrub the bleach into the surface. It's not necessary to use too much pressure; just scrub back and forth until the bleach seems to be taking hold evenly.

Equalizing the bleach

Sometimes, despite your best efforts, the bleach just refuses to take evenly across the surface of the wood. Some spots remain darker in tone than others. If you run into a condition like this, merely apply extra coats of bleach (with proper drying times in between) to the darker areas. Most of the time you'll be able to lighten them enough to wind up with an even-toned surface.

The final step

All of these treatments will raise the grain of the wood. Sand it once more, using a very fine abrasive paper. Just make sure the wood is completely dry before sanding. This may take a day or more under certain conditions.

TYPES OF BLEACH

Laundry bleach

Ordinary household laundry bleach is the mildest chemical you can use, and yet it's surprisingly effective for light-to-moderate bleaching action. Flow the material full-strength onto the surface with a brush, and if necessary scrub it into the wood so that it bleaches evenly. As with all bleach, you have to let the surface dry before you can see the effect. If you want, you can repeat the bleach treatment several times to get greater lightening of the wood. You do not have to neutralize laundry bleach.

Oxalic acid

Oxalic acid comes in the form of fine crystals like sugar or salt. You can buy it in paint stores and most hardware stores. To prepare a usable solution, pour hot water into a glass, porcelain or enamel container. Add the oxalic acid little by little, stirring continuously until no more of it will dissolve in the water. As a general guide, it will take three to four tablespoons per cup of water to reach this condition. Exact proportions aren't really critical.

Mop the solution onto the surface, allow it to dry, and check the tone. If you want to lighten the surface even more, try a second or third coat. Touch up problem areas by scrubbing with steel wool if the bleach is not working evenly.

Oxalic acid is a fairly potent material, so you must test it on scrap wood first. At times it may bleach the scrap wood more than you want. If this is the case, dilute the solution with water to make a milder chemical.

Oxalic acid must be neutralized before you go on to the next step of finishing. For this purpose use a solution of borax. Mix one cup of borax with one quart of hot water. When the borax is completely dissolved, swab the solution onto the surface of the wood, covering all the areas that have been treated with bleach. Rinse the wood with clear water and let dry.

Multi-solution bleach

This is the most powerful bleach available. As a matter of fact, chemicals like this are usually left to professionals. However, the careful amateur should have no trouble at all; just make sure you follow the safety precautions detailed in this chapter. In addition, do follow any special instructions you may find on the container.

Materials of this type usually need a two- or three-part application process. Mix the chemicals according to the instructions on the label. Apply the first solution to the wood with the clean white cloth (wearing rubber gloves, of course). Allow the surface to dry for ten minutes. Then apply the second solution. This time allow the surface to dry overnight—twelve hours is even better.

Check the results. If the surface is not light enough, swab on another coat of the second solution. You can repeat this step (with proper drying times in between so that you can effectively evaluate results) until the wood is chalky white—if that's what you want.

In the case of a three-part bleach, the process may consist of three steps. Other brands of this material are formulated so that you mix different quantities of chemicals in the second and third solutions to adjust the strength of the bleach. All this information is detailed on the label of the container. Make sure you read it carefully.

As with other types of bleach, the chemicals must be neutralized. In this case use ordinary white vinegar diluted with an equal amount of water. Scrub the vinegar solution into the wood with steel wool. Be sure to rub with the grain. Allow the surface to dry completely.

STAINING 7

THERE ARE TWO reasons for staining wood. The first is to enhance the surface. In the finishing trade it's called "bringing out the natural beauty." Actually, the idea is not too outlandish. Some fine cabinet woods such as walnut don't look particularly rich in an unadorned state, and so to give them a more luxurious appearance, stain is used on the wood (for example, walnut stain on walnut wood). The grain becomes vibrant, the richness of the wood becomes apparent, and walnut emerges as real walnut.

The other reason for staining is to upgrade the wood. For example, some people will utilize stain in an effort to upgrade walnut so that it resembles mahogany. In the viewpoint of other craftsmen, this is heresy. However, some woods do make the transition fairly easily. Birch, for example, can be stained and treated to resemble many other types of wood, and the disguise is sometimes quite successful.

The general idea of staining is to color the wood while allowing the grain and tone of the natural material to show through. For that reason almost all stains are transparent to varying degrees. Coatings that cover up completely are more on the order of paint, and these are sometimes used for a kind of mock staining. The process is called graining and involves completely coating the wood with a background tone and then, after this is dry, lightly wiping on a pattern of "wood grain" in a slightly different shade. The final effect can vary between charming and nauseating.

TYPES OF STAIN

Although the forms in which stain is available are varied and many, most of them fall within a few general categories.

Water stains

Water stains consist of dye dissolved in water. This material has many advantages. It's extremely transparent, it's the cheapest of all stains, and it gives a permanent color that resists the effects of sun and other natural bleaching elements. Water stain is relatively easy to handle, although it cannot be smoothed or wiped, once it's on the surface. If you're looking for brilliant colors, this may be the ideal choice.

Unfortunately, along with these happy aspects, there are some disadvantages. Because it is mixed with water, this stain will definitely raise the grain of the wood. This means more smoothing before applying the surface finish. Since water doesn't evaporate so quickly as other materials, it's a good idea to allow a twenty-four-hour drying period after each coat. Application can sometimes be a little bit tricky. Because stain does not blend in, it must be washed on carefully, or you will see stripes. You must always work with the surface wet. It's especially important to complete one surface at a time. Overlaps where two sections meet can cause a noticeable dark line.

Alcohol stains

Alcohol stains are not quite so brilliant in color as water stains and slightly less permanent, but they have one powerful advantage: They dry very quickly. This means that you can finish the job rapidly and go on to the next phase of it without a prolonged waiting period.

On the other hand, the rapid drying can also be a definite disadvantage. Plan to work with the utmost speed so that you can coat an entire surface before it dries, or you will definitely have a problem with lap marks. As with water stains, always work with a wet surface, and plan to brush the material from a dry section toward the last previously covered area. Although alcohol stains do raise the grain of the wood, the effect is not nearly so pronounced as with water-based stains. Still, you may have to sand the surface lightly to make it smooth.

Non–grain-raising stain

Known in the trade as NGR, this material can be made with either alcohol or water. In addition, it has another ingredient that keeps it from raising the grain of the wood. In drying time, it's midway between alcohol and water, and it is considerably more expensive than either. Also, the range of colors available is much more limited.

Although the non–grain-raising aspects are a decided plus, this material has one drawback that sometimes makes craftsmen shy away from it. It has a tendency to overemphasize the grain of the wood. In other words, the soft portions of the wood will absorb more of the stain and come up much darker in color than the hard portions. Sometimes this doesn't make much difference. However, for a material such as fir, where the zebra grain is a problem anyway, NGR stains should not be used.

Oil stains

Oil stains are the old-time materials. Until chemistry took a big hand in furniture finishing, these stains were the only ones around. As the name indicates, the material consists of dye in oil. The colors tend to fade more than those in other types of stain. Although still on the shelves, oil stains are not enjoying the popularity they once held.

Wiping stain

Some cabinetmakers don't even consider wiping stain a stain. They think of it as a paint. It tends to be opaque, except when applied in very thin layers. You may want to consider wiping stain if you are applying a "pickled" or similar finish designed to emphasize the grain of the wood. This is most often used on such materials as oak. In thicker layers, it will serve to hide the grain of the wood. It's useful if you're trying to fake a finish or upgrade a simple wood to a fancier wood. Certainly it's nothing to use on good wood, because in this case there's no need to mask the grain.

Wiping stains are available in a wide variety of forms, including paste, thick liquid and aerosol foam. Many novice craftsmen are taken in by the material because it is so easy to apply and blend. However, the final effect is rarely as pleasing as that of some of the other stains just described.

Mix-your-own

Since the composition of stain is not really very complicated, you may want to mix some according to your own specifications. Surprisingly enough, only a few colors are needed to form the basis of most wood stains. These are, for the most part, earth tones. You can buy them in small tubes right off the shelf of any paint store or artist's supply house. Ask for tinting colors; these may be oil paints or other pigments, but it will always say on the label that they can be used in finishes.

You can use shellac, varnish, or almost any other finish as the vehicle to carry the color. However, here is the formula that many craftsmen utilize, and it's worth trying if you're going to mix up your own stain. Mix one part of polymerized linseed oil with three parts of paint thinner. Mix into this combination the colors you want. Make up a small quan-

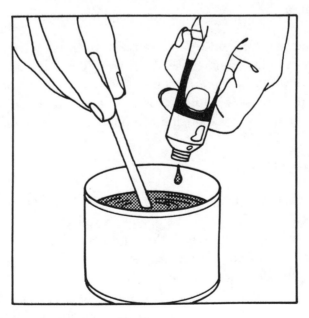

Fig. 29. Mixing your own color of stain.

tity, keeping a record of the amount of each pigment you add, and test the mixture on a piece of scrap wood. There is at least a good chance that you will come up with a very pleasing combination.

For the colors, try burnt umber and burnt sienna mixed in equal quantities. Another variation is burnt umber and yellow ochre. Some furniture finishers swear by burnt sienna and yellow ochre. Or try all three. Mix them in various proportions. You can also use raw umber and raw sienna. There's one other color that you might want to add to the mixture, and that is ordinary white. It has the effect of softening the color. Use it sparingly, and, as always, test out the mixture on a piece of scrap wood before you use it on the furniture.

There is one further combination that is regarded as highly effective. Use penetrating sealer as a vehicle. Add an oil stain to it in the same combinations of earth colors (raw and burnt sienna and umber). If you are going to be working on a wood such as maple, you may want to try adding a bit of orange color; for cherry, try a trace of red. Always, always test. There is at least a fair chance that you may have to dump out the entire batch of material and start over, but that's no great loss. It's all rather inexpensive, and the process of mixing and trying is pure fun.

HOW TO USE STAIN

Test first

Quite frankly, there is no way to predetermine the results you're going to get with any one combination of stain and wood. You just have to try it out and see. For that reason, always test any stain on a piece of scrap wood of the same type as the piece you're treating. If you can't find an acceptable match in scrap wood, then start the work on an unobtrusive part of the furniture. Sometimes the underside of a chair seat will do for test purposes. Also available are the insides of drawer fronts and the undersides of tabletops.

Working conditions

Staining can be done in relatively comfortable surroundings. Just be careful about splatters on walls and floors. Sufficient working room and a dropcloth are about all you will need. For materials, you'll need the stain itself, a brush, and more clean wiping rags than you ever believed existed.

Be sure to wear rubber gloves, not so much to protect yourself against injury—there are no really dangerous chemicals in the materials you will be using—as to guard against stained fingers. Most of the coloring agents are designed to add a permanent hue to wood. On your skin, they do pretty nearly the same thing, and that's not quite so desirable.

Preparations for staining

The wood should be clean and smooth. If there are any irregularities in the surface, they will catch and hold excess stain. That means the material will penetrate at a different rate, and as a result you'll have an unevenness in the color. What's worse, any scratches or mars in the surface will be emphasized. So don't skimp on the sanding. Make sure the surface is completely free of all old finish, wax, grease, or anything else. If any of this remains, the stain will not penetrate evenly. It will take irregularly and leave gaps in the coloration. The only remedy in either case is to bleach out the stain, sand the wood completely smooth, and start all over again. Since this procedure is enough to break one's heart, it pays to do the job properly the first time around.

General hints

Select the brush used to apply stain carefully. The ferrule or middle band around the top part of the bristles should be made of plastic, rubber, or brass. Other types of metals can cause irregular coloration as they react with the chemicals in the stain. Don't use natural bristles for this job. Synthetic bristles seem to hold up better.

Always buy or mix enough stain to complete the job. It is almost impossible to match the color exactly if you run out halfway through.

Start work on an unobtrusive section of the furniture first to learn how this particular wood will take the stain. If all goes well, you can graduate to work on a more visible surface.

Stop only at natural points. In other words, do an entire surface before taking a break. Otherwise, when you begin again after the stain has started to dry, it's hard to avoid dark lap marks that mar an even flow of tone. Keep the surface horizontal if at all possible. This means that you should plan to turn the furniture as you work so the working surface is always facing up. If you do have to work on a vertical surface, plan to start at the bottom and brush upward. You'll get a more even effect, because the stain won't dribble down over an uncoated section of the furniture.

Coat the wood in a series of parallel stripes, overlapping each one slightly. Start each segment so that you brush toward the area previously covered. In other words, you're brushing from a dry section toward a wet one. This technique helps hide lap marks.

If you're not exactly certain of the proper tone, use a stain that is lighter than required. Gradually build up to the shade you want in successive coats. You'll have better control if you do two or more light coats rather than trying to achieve the final effect with one darker layer.

Fig. 30. Always brush stain from a dry section toward a wet one.

As you work, if light spots show up, concentrate on them a little bit more to adjust the flow of color. If you are willing to spend a little more time on this aspect of the work, you can wind up with perfectly even color from one edge to another.

In the case of wood that has a pronounced grain, such as oak, you may have to force the stain into the pores of the wood. Some of the slightly thicker stains tend to remain on the surface. In this case, apply the stain with a stubby-bristle brush. Brush across the grain first, and then finish up the job by brushing in the same direction as the grain.

It is possible to lighten a stained coating that has gone darker than you wanted it to be. Use the proper solvent for the stain you have applied (check the label). Brush it on, then wipe the wood immediately with a clean rag.

How to apply water and alcohol stains

Water and alcohol stains are applied in the same way. Both are very thin, so they flow onto the wood easily and soak right into it. To facilitate an even application, use a big brush or, better yet, a small mop. If you can find one of the old-fashioned string mops used for dish-washing, it's suitable for the purpose.

When you test the stain before applying it to the furniture, dilute it until it creates a color slightly lighter than what you want for the final effect. Then you can have a little more control. A second layer of the stain will generally darken the surface to the color you want.

If the coating is uneven, there is one possible remedy for smoothing it out. Wipe the surface with a cloth soaked in water (in the case of a water stain) or a mixture of water and alcohol (for alcohol stains). Don't expect too much of this procedure, however; it's a sort of last-ditch effort.

Because these materials raise the grain of the wood, allow the furniture to dry at least overnight, and then sand the surface lightly with very fine sandpaper.

How to apply non–grain-raising stains

Apply this material with a brush or a wiping cloth. If it seems to be too thick for easy handling, thin it with alcohol until it flows onto the wood smoothly. As with the other stains, two lighter coats carefully controlled are almost always better than one heavy coat.

How to apply oil stains

If you decide to use this traditional material, use a rag to wipe it on. Allow it to soak in until you see the first hints that it is beginning to dry. Then rub it thoroughly to remove the excess. Do not allow any of the material to remain on the surface. If you don't work quickly enough and there are some gummy spots left, use a little bit of paint thinner on a rag to soften this layer and just wipe the spots away.

How to apply wiping stain

It's a shame this material does not give a truly great finish. It's so easy to apply. Just flow it onto the surface, and work it back and forth with a rag until the entire area of wood is evenly coated. Then wipe off the excess. Since this material is very heavily loaded with pigment, it's very important that none of it remain on the surface. If some does remain, give the surface a final cleanup with a rag lightly moistened with solvent.

How to apply penetrating sealer stain

Brush or mop this material onto the surface. Keep applying it until no more of the liquid soaks into the surface. At this point the wood is saturated, and there will be a layer of liquid on the surface. Let it remain in place for about ten minutes. Then, using paper towels, wipe off the liquid and swab the wood surface to remove moisture. Allow the stain to dry in a warm room; four hours is usually long enough, but overnight is generally safer. Rub the surface with 3/0 steel wool, dust it thoroughly, and apply two or three thin coats of paste wax, buffing each layer well.

At this point you have more than just a stain. You have actually completed the finishing of the piece itself. What you have is a treatment that has penetrated the surface to encompass the fibers of the wood. However, this finish won't have much of a surface "skin" on it. If you are not happy with it, better stick to some of the other finishing schedules in this book.

A pickled or limed finish accentuates the grain of the wood. A contrasting-colored filler—usually white or silver—is applied to the wood and is topped with a clear finish. This is most effective on open-grained woods. *See page 166.*

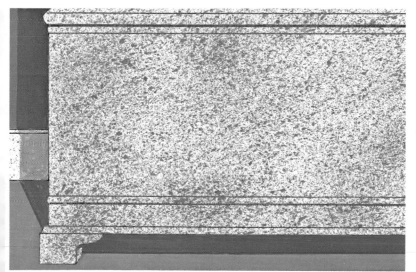

A spatter finish is great for nondescript furniture. It adds a certain flair for a soft but eye-catching effect. The application is genuinely fun and is easy enough for children to do. Here two spatter colors were used over a white base coat. *See page 163.*

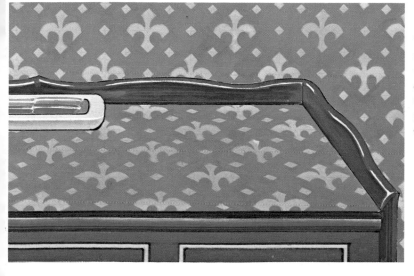

The wallpaper used as the surface of this desk is the same as the paper on the walls. Used with restraint, the combination can be highly decorative. The application is simple: Just glue the wallpaper down and put a clear finish on top. *See page 159.*

This old night table seemed almost past saving. Many of the joints were loose, the veneer was peeling off in spots, and the hardware had long since disappeared. Also, the finish was badly checked and was actually flaking off, exposing the wood in spots.

After the old paint was removed, the natural wood underneath proved to be well worth restoring. The joints were reglued, and the loose veneer was fastened down into place. A thorough sanding with a medium and then a fine abrasive gave a soft patina to the well-seasoned old wood.

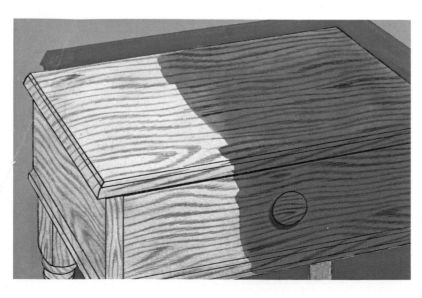

Staining fulfills the promise of the original piece. In this case, the wood tone is brushed onto the surface and wiped off, and it actually enhances the grain and color of the wood itself. When the staining is completed, several coats of a clear finish will be applied.

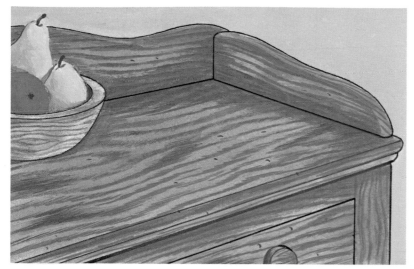

Highlighting simulates the effect that years and years of care can create. Note how the coloration is darker in the corners and crevices than it is along the edges or flat surfaces. This would happen naturally if the piece of furniture were dusted, waxed and polished over a period of many years. *See page 156.*

A fake grained finish is easy to create if you have a deft hand and a bit of imagination. A light ground color was applied to the chest shown here. When it was completely dry, the graining pigment was brushed on top, and the swirled pattern was created with a graining comb. *See page 169.*

In some settings a color dye can turn a piece of furniture into an effective and charming decorative accent. A fabric dye was applied to this chest of drawers and topped with a clear finish. The grain of the wood still shows through. *See page 141.*

Sampling of available finishes. Consult your hardware or paint store for a more complete selection.

SEALER AND FILLER 8

ALTHOUGH SEALER and filler are generally spoken of together, they really handle entirely separate tasks in the routine of furniture finishing. Since both are quite essential, we'll discuss them one at a time.

SEALER

The traditional material used for sealing is clear shellac. It is still used today because it does the work in a very efficient manner. However, shellac can be a rather temperamental material unless you follow a few simple rules.

Buy in small quantities. Get just enough to finish each job, and discard any left over when you're finished. Always buy shellac at a large store that specializes in finishing materials. Such a shop will have a large turnover, so the stock will probably be fresh. Shellac does not hold up very well when left on the shelf for a long time.

To use shellac as a sealer, buy what is called four-pound cut. This is a technical term that describes a particular thickness of the shellac. For use as a sealer, shellac has to be very thin. To prepare a solution, mix one pint of shellac with eight pints of denatured alcohol. Keep the solution in a glass jar with a tightly sealed lid.

If you prefer, you can also buy a commercial sealer. This has the advantage of a much longer shelf life, so you can keep it around from one job to the next. Be sure to read the instructions on the label. Quite likely the material will have to be thinned with lacquer thinner, but if there are different directions, be sure to follow them. Also, be certain to read all the information on the label. Some types of commercial sealers are intended for spray application only. Results can be unhappy if you try to brush this material on.

Despite the name, clear shellac is not really clear but slightly amber in color. Of course, if it is used in very diluted form as a sealer, it's unlikely that you'll be able to notice the very fine difference in color caused by the amber tint—unless you're going to use a very light finish on very light wood. In this case buy what's known as water-white shellac. It has no amber tone at all.

The purpose of sealer is to keep coats of finish from interfering or "bleeding" into each other. It also serves to seal the surface of the wood to keep the finish from continually soaking into it. This, then, allows the finish to build up into a layer on the surface.

Application is simple and fast. Merely brush on the sealer with a soft brush, using a fast stroke. No need for fancy brushwork; just make the coating as even as possible.

Shellac and shellac-based sealers are naturally fast-drying materials. When they are in a very diluted form, the action is even faster. Most of the time the coating at one end of the piece will be completely dry before you can finish applying it to the other end.

FILLER

Filler performs a very essential function: It fills in the pores of the wood to make a smooth surface. This helps the finish take evenly and level out into a flat layer without indicating the grain underneath. Almost all woods need some filler. Birch, maple and other woods that have a subtle grain require only a thin liquid-type filler. Woods with a pronounced grain, such as walnut, mahogany, oak and chestnut, need a heavy paste-type filler in order to fill in the open pores. Liquid filler is the consistency of coffee cream. On the other hand, paste filler is a thick, ugly mass. Furthermore, it separates in the container and must be mixed well. The easiest variety of filler to use, at least for the amateur, is a type known as "sylex." You'll find this identification somewhere on the label. Professional furniture finishers sometimes use more exotic materials for this purpose, but these make unnecessary complications for the average craftsman.

Be sure to thin the paste-type filler before using it. Mix it thoroughly, and then, following the instructions on the label, add a liquid until you wind up with a material that's about the consistency of whipping cream. In most cases, turpentine is used for thinning, but do read the instructions carefully, since other materials are sometimes preferred.

Filler divides into two main categories. There's the type designed to be used before the wood is stained, and a different type to be used after the wood has already been toned. The difference is in the color of the material, not in the consistency or content. If you are going to apply the filler before you stain the wood, buy the material in a natural wood tone. Later, if you do any staining, you can stain both the wood and the filler at one time. If you're going to apply filler after the wood has already been stained, buy filler that is the approximate shade of the final finish or slightly darker.

Preparations

The surface of the wood that is going to be filled should be sanded perfectly smooth and should be completely free of paint, dust, dirt, oil, and old finish.

To seal the raw wood, brush a very thin coat of sealer onto it. This is called a wash coat. Be careful that it doesn't puddle up, or you will fill in the depressions of the grain and not leave enough room for the filler.

Applying filler

You can cover the surface of a small piece of furniture all at one time. However, if you're going to be working on a large area, plan to cover only a two-foot section at one time. Completely finish the segment before you go on to the next two-foot section. Stir the filler before you begin to apply it, and repeat the stirring several times during the process. It's quite heavy and has a tendency to settle.

Use a stubby brush to apply filler. An old worn one will do splen-

Fig. 31. Applying filler with a stubby brush.

didly. If you don't have one, merely cut down a new brush (a very cheap one, of course) until the bristles are only two or three inches long.

Application is anything but an arty process. It is, in the jargon of the professional trade, "real slob work." Dunk the bristles into the filler and brush across the grain. The word *brush* does not really describe the process. It's more like scrubbing. The idea is to work the bristles back and forth across the grain so that you actually scrub the material into the pores of the wood. Use a brush full of filler. When the pores seem to be completely filled, stroke across the grain with a full brush, and finally brush lightly in the direction of the grain. The purpose of this whole routine is to fill the pores of the wood, and standard brushwork does not seem to accomplish this purpose.

The final effect after all this work is disastrous. The coating will be sloppy, uneven, messy, and most unattractive. The next ingredient required is patience. Keep an eye on the filler while you wait. At one point the surface shine will disappear, and the filler will appear dull. This is your cue to start cleaning off the excess. The only critical aspect in using filler is the timing for this phase of the work. If you start to clean too soon, you will work the filler right out of the pores of the wood. If you

Fig. 32. Using burlap to remove excess filler.

Fig. 33. Squeegeeing off excess filler with plastic.

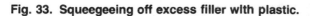

wait until it's too late, the material will be tacky and hard to work with, and the filler will once more tend to pull out of the depressions in the wood.

There are several ways to remove the excess filler. If you can find lots of burlap bags, they'll be fine for the job. Use them to scrub, working across the grain of the wood. Change to a clean section of the burlap whenever necessary.

Another technique is to squeegee the surface coating away, using pieces of stiff, straight cardboard or a strip of straightedge plastic. The plastic will be more efficient, but the cardboard is far safer. The idea is to remove the excess material from the surface without damaging the wood underneath. Again, all the action should be cross-grained so there's no tendency to pull the material out of the pores of the wood.

After removing most of the excess filler, finish by rubbing with burlap, as in the first method.

If you handle the task successfully, the wood surface will be completely free of filler, while the filler remains evenly in the pores of the wood. Allow the surface to dry for twenty-four hours before continuing with the finishing routine. After the material is dry, smooth the surface with very, very fine sandpaper, and apply another coat of sealer.

Part III
Finishing
Your Furniture

WAX FINISHES 9

FOR A LOT OF practical reasons, wax is not a very good finish for furniture. It's soft; it has virtually no resistance to scratches and abrasion; and anything at all will mar the surface, including alcohol and water. Nor can it stand up to the wear and tear of daily living.

And yet, wax is a very popular finish—and rightfully so. The reason is simple: A wax finish is beautiful. Properly applied, it will give a soft, warm luster to wood that can rarely be matched by any chemical compound out of the laboratory. It's also easy to repair. A little more wax, a little more buffing, and most damage seems to fade away.

A good wax finish appears to build up depth, acquiring a lustrous quality that extends right down into the wood. Then, too, with age it builds up a soft patina that seems to glow with its own deep, inner light. Certainly for antiques there are few things better than a well-buffed wax finish to bring out the traditional feeling of the piece.

Preparations

The wood should be sanded to a glossy smoothness, and the surface should be completely dry and free of grease, stains and debris. The wood should also be bleached and stained (if necessary), and all imperfections should be repaired and the grain filled.

Because this is a completely rubbed finish, you won't need to worry nearly so much about dust-free working conditions. Nor will fumes be a problem. Both the sealers used for the finishing schedules and the wax itself are nontoxic to breathe.

In general, it is not a good idea to apply any type of wax to bare wood. While this may be permissible on some of the hard woods such as birch or walnut, it can be relatively disastrous on a soft wood such as pine. Dirt and grime may become embedded in the surface. Then they will move through the layer of wax and will actually become embedded deep in the finish. When this happens there is virtually no way to clean the finish. Even removing the wax may not work, because the dirt may be actually nestling among the fibers of the wood itself.

For this reason, a sealer coat is almost always essential underneath a wax finish. Although shellac is good for this, there are penetrating sealers that are especially designed to go with the wax finish. Application is easy (see page 124). When the surface is dry, you can start to work with the wax.

Some of the penetrating sealers also contain stain, so that two phases of the work can be done at one time. This does, however, bring up a choice. There are two ways to apply a wax finish: You can either stain the wood surface first, and then put a clear wax on top, or you can use no stain, but apply a colored wax instead.

For convenience, many home craftsmen prefer to use a stain or stained sealer. However, if you want to mix up your own colored wax or use the softly mottled procedure described later on, do not use stain, and make sure the sealer is clear.

Wax

Paste wax

Use paste wax made especially for furniture finishing. It's available in most hardware and all paint stores. Although some special liquid-type waxes are available, paste waxes are better and much more popular. Do not, under any circumstances, use a liquid self-polishing floor wax or any of the other preparations containing wax that are sold for home use. This is an entirely different type of material and won't do at all for furniture finishing.

Be sure to follow any special instructions you find on the label of the container. For example, some waxes should be applied with a damp cloth. In this case, merely wet a cloth, wring it out until it is damp, and apply the wax with it. This seems to make the wax spread more easily.

Mix your own wax

If you have a special color in mind that is not available ready-mixed in either stain or wax, you can make your own colored wax by adding the exact tints and shades you want to clear wax. The procedure is relatively simple and quite a bit of fun. Take the lid off the can of clear paste wax and dig out two or three tablespoons of the wax to make room for the color and to allow space for stirring. Melt the remaining wax right in the can. Be extremely careful when you do this. Do not under any circumstances put the can of wax directly on a heating source—gas or electric—or on a direct flame. Instead use the hot-water-bath method. Put a pan of hot water on the stove and set the can of wax in it. The water

Fig. 34. The hot-water-bath method of mixing wax.

level should be just below the rim of the can. Keep the water just barely simmering, and gradually the wax will melt into a liquid.

There are several different materials you can use for tinting clear wax. Ordinary wax crayons are one. You can also buy special wax-coloring materials in paint stores or hobby shops. However, most craftsmen use ordinary artists' oil paints. The most popular colors used are various combinations of burnt umber, burnt sienna, raw sienna, raw umber, and yellow ochre.

Keep several factors in mind when you mix up the wax. For one thing, it will be hard to get a deep color in the final finish, because the layer of wax is relatively thin. For this reason you have to mix it up considerably darker than seems advisable. Do keep in mind, however, that you are going to build up several layers of wax to achieve the finish. The color will become deeper as the various coats are applied one on top of the other.

The best procedure is to test the mixture as you go along. Just dip out a bit of the melted wax and allow it to cool. Then apply the material to a section of the wood you are going to finish. Usually you can find some hidden area for a test, such as the underside of a chair or the inside of a drawer front. If necessary apply several layers of the wax, allowing drying time and proper buffing between the coats, before you make your final decision about color. Keep juggling and adjusting tints and shades until you make the melted wax the exact tone you want. Then remove the container from the water bath and allow it to cool until the wax is once again the consistency of a soft paste.

Softly mottled finish

There's one other technique that until now has been a closely held secret among professional furniture finishers. You may have seen an old tabletop that seems to have a subtlety or movement to the color. It's nothing you can put your finger on; however, the shade, the tone, the feel seems to vary ever so slightly from one section to the other. If you have ever been fortunate enough to see any antique paneling in museum homes, you have seen this.

The how-to of it all is surprisingly simple. You will need two types of wax: clear and colored. Dig a bit of each out of the containers and place the waxes side by side on a flat, smooth surface. Both of these are

Fig. 35. Mixing wax for a softly mottled finish.

still in paste form; there is no need to soften or heat them. With a small putty knife, add a little of the colored wax to the pile of clear wax. Cut through the pile several times with the putty knife. It will be impossible to blend the two perfectly, but they should be fairly well mixed. If the final tone is not dark enough, add more of the colored wax and keep cutting through the pile.

You'll finally wind up with a large lump of mixed wax. For the most part, it will be fairly even toned, except that there will be tiny pockets of both clear wax and colored wax scattered liberally throughout. If you apply this material to the wood, an interesting thing happens. Most of the wood will have a relatively even tone; however, every now and then there will be a tiny streak of darker wax or a streak of the clear wax. The first layer won't look too impressive, because the mottling will be far too pronounced. But after you have allowed this layer to dry thoroughly and have buffed it well, you're ready for the second layer. When you have applied three or four coats, you will begin to achieve the soft, mottled look that was the purpose of the whole routine.

General rules for applying wax

Always apply several thin layers of wax. One thick coating will become a sticky mess that's hard or impossible to buff.

Never treat an area larger than two or three square feet at one time, unless you're going to buff the coating with a motor-driven power brush (as described below). This means that you can do the top of a small chest all at once, but a dining table will have to be done in several segments.

Smooth on several layers of wax, allowing each to dry thoroughly. Do not try to buff the wax while it is still wet. This is a waste of energy as well as wax. When a layer is dry, buff it thoroughly until the coating has a soft sheen. If you are working by hand, use a soft fiber shoe brush first, and then shift to a lamb's wool buffer for the final polish.

You can save a lot of energy by using a power-buffer. In this case use a tampico brush or a lamb's wool polishing bonnet hooked up to the chuck of a quarter-inch electric drill or a standard polishing tool. However, for best results still do the first phase of the buffing by hand, using a soft fiber shoe brush.

Fig. 36. Buffing wax with a tampico brush.

The very best power brush for this job is a circular one that hooks into the chuck of a quarter-inch electric drill or flexible shaft. This attachment has the same bristles as the shoeshine brush, except that they are longer and arranged in a circular pattern. With it, you can do both the hand buffing and the final polishing at one time.

When you're using a power tool, you can coat larger areas of wood with wax before beginning the buffing. You still must apply very thin layers of wax, however.

There's no need to wait after you have buffed one layer of wax before applying the next. You only have to make sure the wax is dry before you begin to buff. Otherwise, especially with a power-driven fiber brush, you run the risk of removing most of the wax in the polishing operation.

Letting the tone flow

Because you are building up the tone and shading in several layers, there's an unusual opportunity with wax to get a flow or movement of the wood tones. This can be especially useful when you have a large expanse of wood to cover. The best example would be paneling along one or two walls of a room. In such a case you can gradually change the coloring formula of the wax as you work. If you are using the softly mottled technique, for example, you can simply add a bit more color every now and then as you go. In this way you will have a very interesting, almost imperceptible flow of the coloration that can be exceedingly handsome in its final effect.

The old-time colonial builders were aware of this technique and its possibilities. They used it quite effectively, for example, in toning the wood wall running alongside a flight of stairs. It is, as you'll discover, a most interesting decorating possibility to have up your sleeve.

BRUSH FINISHES 10

SHELLAC

ALTHOUGH SHELLAC HAS BEEN around for a long time, it still has a lot of good things going for it. Tradition is only one. Back in the early days of cabinetmaking, shellac was a popular and highly respected finish. It was used in the clear form that's still around today. In addition, the old-time cabinetmakers used to add different pigments to the basic material. All that this took was a tint that could be dissolved in alcohol. Of all the tones and shades, black was perhaps the most popular. It formed the basic undercoat for such well-known antiques as Hitchcock chairs; the traditional stenciling went on top of the shellac.

Shellac continued to be used until better finishes came along. Science has pretty much passed shellac by, and now there are many new materials that give much the same effect but with better properties. However, for small objects, where fast drying is an advantage, or as a sealer coat, shellac is still valuable. For large-scale finishing work, you have to decide for yourself whether to use it. Shellac has very good adhesion, is flexible enough to withstand some slight movement of the surface underneath and is pretty good at resisting abrasion (it's still used as a floor finish by many landlords). On the other hand, too many things affect it, including water, alcohol, and most other liquids.

How to buy shellac

Fresh is the key word. As we've said before, shellac does not last very long on the shelf. For this reason, buy it only at a large store that appears to have a rapid turnover of stock, and buy only enough for one job at a time. Discard the balance when the work is completed unless you know for sure that you will be doing more finishing within a week.

If at any point you are tempted to use shellac that has been sitting around for a while, be sure to test it first. That's the only way you can make certain that the material will still dry to a hard, non-tacky surface. Just brush some of it out onto a piece of scrap wood. If it tends to remain gummy, do not use it under any circumstances. The material is probably too old, and you will have nothing but trouble.

Shellac is sold in two forms: white or orange. White shellac is relatively clear, although it will give a slight amber cast to the surface. Orange shellac, especially when it is used in a multicoat finish, results in a decidedly amber, almost orange, cast. So if you are applying shellac to a dark wood or trying to match an antique finish (the old-timers used orange shellac), the darker material will do. For other applications, stick with the white kind.

Proper dilution is important

Shellac generally has to be diluted before it is used. The shellac that you buy is classified by its dilution, or "cut." The thickness or thinness of the cut is identified by the term "pound."

The pound simply refers to the amount of dry shellac by weight that is dissolved into one gallon of denatured alcohol to make the cut that you buy or use. In other words, if one pound of dry shellac is dissolved in one gallon of alcohol, you will wind up with a very thin shellac known as one-pound cut.

Since you can't thicken shellac very easily but can always dilute it, you will probably find it handiest to buy it in the thickest cut that you plan to use. You can purchase some shellac thinner or alcohol at the same time, so that you can dilute the shellac to a thinner material whenever desired.

It's all done by mathematical calculations. Assuming that you are starting with three-pound-cut shellac, you can transform it into two-pound cut (which is a medium-consistency material) by mixing on the basis of five parts shellac to two parts of alcohol. Continuing down the scale to the thinnest material that you would possibly use as a finish, you can get one-pound cut by diluting three parts of shellac (again the three-pound-cut kind) with four parts of alcohol. Of course, you don't have to dilute shellac yourself; you can buy it ready mixed in any cut you want.

The three-pound-cut shellac is used as it comes from the container only for such projects as finishing floors. This is about as thick as you can use without dilution. If it is any heavier, it will ooze from the brush like molasses. You must decide which cut of shellac to use. The thin types such as a one-pound cut are generally forgiving of mistakes. The shellac tends to level out. It goes on smoothly, and you won't have any trouble with runs, sags or wrinkles. On the other hand, it will take a good many coats of this material to build up any kind of respectable skin or surface on the wood. That means more coats to brush on, plus more drying and sanding time between layers.

If you're learning, do start off with the one-pound cut. While it's true that you will have a little bit more labor, you are not likely to make any serious mistakes.

Finishing schedule

Remember, this is not a one-coat process. In order to get a decent shellac finish, you will have to build up a surface by brushing on several layers. Following the instructions already given, purchase the shellac and dilute it to the proper consistency.

Surface preparations

As with almost every other finish, the wood should be clean, dry, and grease-free. It should also be carefully smoothed, stained, filled, and probably sealed. In other words, you are working with a surface that is now ready for the top layer or skin.

Fig. 37. The correct way to load a brush with shellac.

Applying shellac

Don't try to use a cheap, skimpy brush. You will need a good one with lots of bristles so that you can load it with shellac. Try to get away from the habit of scraping the dipped bristles across the lip of the can. Instead, pat the brush against the side of the can on the inside, then quickly upend the brush and shift over to the work surface. Then you can flip the brush down into the normal position and start brushing.

Apply a full, flowing coat of shellac, using a smooth, easy motion. There is no need for frantic back-and-forth strokes. Application is an easy, gentle process in which you use a thick brush fully loaded with the finish. On succeeding strokes, work from the dry portion back toward the last previously coated segment. Don't worry about lap marks. Each new coat softens and smooths the layer underneath. When the entire piece has been coated, allow enough drying time; probably one to two hours will do.

Smoothing the finish

Sand the dry, hard shellac coating with a sanding block around which you have wrapped a sheet of very fine abrasive paper. An open grit, silicon carbide paper in a grade of at least 240 is probably best. Do not use flint paper for this job.

The purpose of light sanding at this stage is to eliminate any slight fuzz of wood fibers that may still be present on the surface, and to remove stiffened particles of dust. You are not trying to accomplish any large-scale removal of material, so you will not have to use any heavy muscle.

After sanding, dust the surface carefully (a vacuum cleaner is fine for this job), give it a final once-over with a tack cloth, and then apply the second layer of shellac. Allow the same amount of drying time before you start the sanding process once more.

After the third coat, you can either leave the surface as it is or apply a thin layer of paste wax, buffed to a nice soft sheen. If there still appear to be any irregularities or slightly foreign particles in the finish, rub it down with 4/0 steel wool coated with paste wax. As before, buff it well.

One final tip. Between coats, keep the brush soft by allowing it to soak in a jar of alcohol. Drill a hole through the handle so you can insert a length of coat hanger wire, and keep the bristles dangling off the bottom of the jar. When you are ready to apply the next coat of shellac, merely wipe off the bristles.

VARNISH

Varnish has been around since the days of the clipper ships. There's a lot in its favor, and ruggedness is at the top of the list. A good quality varnish properly applied can shrug off almost anything gentler than battery acid. Obviously, it's completely immune to water, alcohol, and household cleaning solutions. The drawback is that this material is more difficult to apply than many other finishes, tends to dry slowly, and in the process can pick up a lot of dust and miscellaneous particles.

How to buy varnish

Laboratories are producing an increasingly wide variety of varnishes, including acrylic, vinyl and phenolic. As these types of varnishes are used for many different jobs, it's probably wise to buy varnish at a large store staffed by people who know their business and can give advice about specific types of varnish that may not be familiar to you. It's best to get the correct varnish for each specific job you want to tackle.

For example, you may have heard many good things about marine varnish. Sure, it's a great material—for boats. It will withstand an incredible amount of abusive weather. However, it always stays a little bit soft, which is not good for household surfaces. Bar-top varnish is impervious to everything except a machine gun, but it's difficult to apply and tends to dry very slowly.

Although varnish will keep better than shellac, there's really no reason to buy more than you need for a specific project. Also, always allow the container of varnish to rest quietly for a day or so before using it. This gives any bubbles a chance to rise to the surface and burst. Otherwise they tend to incorporate themselves into the finish.

Working conditions

The big problem with varnish, as mentioned before, is dust. Because this finish dries slowly, there's ample time for any dust drifting by to embed itself into the soft finish. For that reason, working conditions are quite important.

Select the area where you are going to finish furniture very carefully. Vacuum it thoroughly and wash down any exposed surfaces. As much as possible, seal off the dust and provide natural ventilation (no great gusts of wind blowing through the area). It's also a good idea to have a picking stick at hand.

Finishing schedule

Surface preparations

The surface of the furniture should be clean, dry, and completely free of grease. The wood should also be smoothed, stained, and filled. Wipe the wood down thoroughly and then go over it once more, using the soft brush attachment of a vacuum cleaner. As a final step, wipe the smooth wood with a tack cloth to pick up the last bits of dust or wood fiber that remain.

Applying varnish

Use a varnish brush for this work. Dip the bristles one-third of the way into the material. Do not scrape them across the rim of the can. Instead, merely press them against the inside of the can to remove the excess varnish. The idea is to eliminate dripping without creating bubbles.

In general, try to arrange the work so that a light shines across the surface toward you. Varnish, by and large, is not a forgiving finish, so it's important that you correct all mars, bare spots, sags and runs as they occur. It's easier to do if you can see the problems.

Thin the first coat of varnish, using one part turpentine to four parts of varnish. This thinner coat seems to penetrate the wood a little better and acts as a sealer for the filler and for the coats that will follow.

As you flow the material on, always work from a dry portion of the wood toward the last coated wet section. Cover each surface in overlapping bands. Do not try to do the entire surface at once. As you complete each band, "tip" the surface, using only the tips of the bristles to allow the brush to merely float over the surface. The idea is to remove any

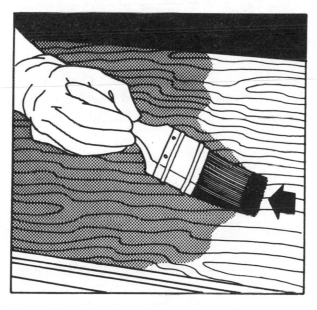

Fig. 38. Flowing varnish onto the surface.

Fig. 39. Tipping the surface.

bubbles and also to level the varnish at the same time. If you skip any areas or notice any minor mars after the surface has begun to harden, do not try to correct them. Instead, wait until the finish is completely dry, sand it lightly, and figure on correcting the damage with the next coat you apply.

Some professional furniture finishers "scrub" the first coat into the wood with a wad of cloth for perfect coverage. If you notice any bubbles appearing in the coat, this is sometimes a wise procedure. In any event, this is something you'll have to do when working on carvings or any other intricate surfaces. After you have coated them, tip each surface carefully to remove runs and bubbles.

It is very important to allow each coat to dry completely. Check the instructions on the label and then add some extra time for security. The usual drying period is from two to three days—but sometimes more. Be sure to allow additional drying time if the weather is humid, because this retards the hardening of the finish. On days that are quite humid, better scratch the entire project, because there's a distinct possibility you might have to wait until next St. Swithin's Day for the surface to finally harden.

It's important to scuff the hardened finish between coats. For this, use a sanding block and a very fine grit abrasive paper. The idea is to give a "tooth" or very slight roughness to the hardened varnish finish so that the next coat will adhere properly.

After the first layer, flow on successive coats of full-strength varnish. The technique is to hold the brush so that it is almost horizontal with the surface. This allows the varnish to almost ooze out in a nice, flat, even layer.

To give the last finish a luster, wait until it is absolutely dry and hard, then rub it with 4/0 steel wool and paste wax. Allow the wax to dry and then buff it for a rich luster.

One final tip. It's not a good idea to apply varnish onto a vertical surface. For best results, always turn the work so that you can work on a level, horizontal area.

POLYURETHANE

Many of the procedures for applying polyurethane are the same as for varnish. As a matter of fact, some finishes that you buy under the name of "varnish" are actually polyurethane, especially those called "plastic varnish."

The actual formulation of the polyurethane depends on the brand. This means that it is especially important to read the instructions on the container carefully before going to work. The manufacturer may have introduced some special techniques of his own to the procedure.

Polyurethane is available as a clear finish as well as in a wide range of colors and wood tones. These are somewhat transparent, so each added layer will intensify the tone or color of the finish. You must test thoroughly on a piece of scrap wood before you begin on the furniture. Remember also to test the effect of several coats so you can foresee the final result.

Since the final surface is so tough, you cannot dull it after it has dried. If you want a matte finish, buy the special kind of polyurethane for this.

Stay away from the industrial polyurethane that comes in two parts. You have to mix them together before applying. You will get splendid results by using the more common single-part material.

Finishing schedule

Make absolutely sure that any of the materials used in various un-dercoating processes (stain, filler, bleach) are bone dry before applying polyurethane. The solvent contained in this coating can "lift" the other materials out of the wood unless they have had the opportunity to dry completely and set.

There is no need to stir, mix or thin polyurethane. Just apply it with a soft brush as it comes from the can. Brush on a full flowing coat that is almost runny. You do not have to use a sealer or undercoat; the first coat of polyurethane takes care of it.

There is one important consideration when applying this material. Since it dries to a very hard, extra-tough surface, succeeding layers may not adhere properly unless you take special precautions. The key to this is timing. You must apply the various coats within the time limit spelled out by the manufacturer on the label of the can.

Here's what happens. If you are on schedule, the solvent in the new coat of polyurethane will slightly soften the coat underneath, and the two will bond together firmly. If you wait too long, there is a chance that the new layer cannot adhere properly to the coat underneath. When this happens, lightly scuff the finish before brushing on the new layer. Use very fine sandpaper for this job, and keep working until you have slightly dulled the finish over the entire area to be coated. Then dust thoroughly and apply the new coat of polyurethane.

There is one unusual aspect to this finish. Because of some quirk in its chemistry, it hardens more rapidly in humid weather than in dry.

LACQUER

Most of the time, brushing lacquer is used right out of the container. (See chapter 11 for applying spraying lacquer.) If you do have to thin it, use only the material recommended on the label (usually lacquer thinner). For the most part, use lacquer as close to the recommended consistency as you can. If it is too thick, it will be hard to brush and may not dry well; if too thin, it will run, and several coats may be needed to build the proper thickness or skin.

The primary problem with brushing on a nice even coat of lacquer is tied in directly to its primary advantage. It's fast drying, so dust, hairs and other materials—even the brush—can get stuck in it. This mixed blessing can work to your benefit, however, if you apply the lacquer properly. Because lacquer has a strong tendency to self-level, brushmarks, slight streaks and even occasional dribbles disappear.

Finishing schedule

Before you use lacquer on it, a wood surface must be smoothed, bleached, stained, filled and sealed, and, most important, absolutely dust-free.

Since lacquer is self-leveling, you do not have to apply it by brushing it back and forth. Merely flow it on with a good-quality soft brush. Load the brush with as much lacquer as it will hold without dripping. Dunk the bristles into the container until about one-third of their length is covered with the lacquer. As you withdraw the brush, tap the bristles lightly on the inside of the can to pat off the excess lacquer.

Hold the brush nearly parallel to the surface of the wood. This allows the lacquer to flow from the brush onto the surface with the least interference. As with most other coatings, work from a dry or uncoated area toward the last previously covered section to eliminate any lap marks.

Although lacquer is one of the fastest drying coatings you can use, always allow plenty of time for each coat to become really hard before brushing on the next layer. Usually, if you can't dent the material with your fingernail, it's safe to proceed. However, check the instructions on the label of the particular lacquer you are using for drying time or for any specific recommendations from the manufacturer.

Scuff each hardened coat with fine steel wool and remove all dust before brushing on the next layer. Lacquer tends to soften or dissolve the layers of lacquer underneath, so that the finish forms a coating that has become one layer. This softening also minimizes any minor errors or unevenness in the finish.

PENETRATING SEALER

Of all available finishes, penetrating sealer is the simplest to apply—bar none! Apply? That's an overstatement. You just slop it on. The important thing is to encourage the wood to absorb as much of it as possible.

Just dunk a cloth or a mop in the penetrating sealer and swab it on the wood. Or, if you have a large surface to cover, pour a small pool of it on a horizontal segment of the wood and work it back and forth with cloth or mop. Keep applying more sealer until the wood will no longer absorb it and there is an even layer of it on top of the surface. Then wait.

Wait for the length of time recommended on the label of the brand of sealer you are using (anywhere from a few minutes to an hour). If any sealer remains on the surface after this time, wipe it off.

Allow this first coat to dry overnight. Then follow the same procedure for the second coat. Generally, sealer does not raise the grain, but if this has happened, you can smooth the surface of the wood with steel wool before applying more penetrating sealer. Allow the second coat of sealer to dry overnight before applying a third, final coat (if it is needed), or wax, oil or whatever you are using for the top coat.

ENAMEL

Enamel is a tough opaque paint that comes in a wonderful assortment of bright colors. Because it is so well known and so readily available, many people think of it as something you slop on the kitchen chairs when you want a fast color change. Not so. Enamel is a high-quality finishing material.

Do start out with really good enamel. Although it is available in a wide price range, the more expensive enamel often gives a tougher surface and is easier to apply.

For the best job, buy fresh enamel and get only enough for the task at hand. Many do-it-yourselfers try to make do with odd bits of leftover enamel, and the result looks like grandmother's old kitchen chairs. If you use good-quality new enamel and apply it according to instructions, you will wind up with a beautiful finishing job.

Enamel must be thoroughly mixed before it is applied. The easiest way is to have the paint store put the container in their power shaker. After a minute or so, most paint is ready for immediate use, even if it has been sitting on the shelf for years.

If you mix the enamel at home, use a technique known as boxing. Open the can and pour off the liquid on top. Stir up the heavy material at the bottom with a clean stick or stirring paddle. When it is all loose and about the consistency of a thick but even paste, pour back some of the liquid. Keep mixing, adding the liquid a bit at a time until it is all back into one can again. By this time, the enamel should be ready to use.

As with many other coatings, you can color enamel yourself. Some paint stores have the colors and the equipment to custom-mix whatever you want. But since you can get a wide variety of shades and tints right off the shelf, you are far better off buying the right color of enamel than trying to get the precise color you want by trial and error.

Finishing schedule

Undercoating is very important with enamel. Seal the smooth, bare, dry, grease-free wood surface with a coat of very thin shellac or a commercial sealer. When this is dry, brush on a coat of the undercoat recommended by the manufacturer. Generally, this is a thin paint. Just brush it on as evenly as possible and don't be concerned that there are thin spots in the surface, the wood shows through in sections, and the color is uneven. Most undercoat comes in one or at most two shades: a light version for use under light shades of enamel and a darker variety for dark tones. Again, follow the manufacturer's recommendation although you can put dark enamel over light undercoat.

Enamel is another "forgiving" finishing material. Unevenness, brush marks and similar minor errors level off before the coating dries. In order to get a layer of paint as even as possible, apply in two steps. First brush on the enamel, working across the grain and then with it. Follow this by "tipping": Hold the brush almost upright, and sweep it lightly across the surface in the direction of the grain. This will help level the surface.

Always work from an uncovered section toward the last area painted. If the piece is relatively small, you may want to coat all of one surface before tipping. When covering a large area, apply enamel to two or three square feet at a time before tipping. Inspect the piece carefully before putting it aside to dry. If any loose brush hairs are embedded in the surface, carefully remove them with a picking stick and lightly tip over the spot to smooth the coating.

Do not skimp on drying time. Enamel should be smooth, hard and tough before succeeding coats are applied. Check the label on the container for specific times, anywhere from a few hours to a day. Depending on weather conditions, some enamels may require several days' drying time. In any event, do not rush this step.

Use very fine sandpaper to scuff each coat of enamel (except the final one) when it is completely hard. The idea is to remove the gloss on the surface so that the next layer will make a firm bond.

SPRAY FINISHES 11

AT THIS WRITING there is some concern over possible damage to the atmosphere done by all those very convenient pressurized spray cans. If it turns out that they do indeed produce ill effects, we will have to give them up. We have learned a great deal from these spray cans, however; they introduced the idea of spray application to virtually every household in the country. So, to a certain extent, most of us have some acquaintance with the idea of handling spray coatings. The equipment, although a bit more complicated than cans, is easy to use.

For some types of finish, spray application is perfect. It's possible to build up a strong, durable finish in a series of thin coats. However, the picture is not entirely bright. The finish that you want to apply must be designed for spray application. Otherwise you can end up with a sticky mess. Also, the particular sprayer you use must have adequate power. Finally, the finish has to be thinned to the precise consistency for spray application.

Not all finishes can be sprayed. If you want to apply a very thick finish, you're in for trouble. It can be done with a heavy-duty spray gun—most of the time. However, this equipment is generally beyond the reach of most home finishers. (If you do want to try professional or heavy-duty equipment, you can rent it from hardware stores or companies that specialize in renting equipment.)

In general, lacquer is best applied with a spray gun. Just make sure you get spray lacquer; lacquer for brush application is considerably thicker and takes much longer to dry. Forget about trying to spray varnish. The finish would be encrusted with bubbles. Enamel can be sprayed if it is thinned for application. Check the label on the container to make sure the material can be applied in this fashion. Shellac? Sure, you can apply it with a spray gun, but why? It's so easy to brush on, and it dries so quickly. Don't bother trying to spray stain. It is designed to be wiped, once it has been applied, to rub the material out into an even coloration. It's not a good idea to spray any of the polyurethane finishes. The equipment is just too hard to clean afterward, and you may wind up with a thoroughly gummed sprayer. As an all-around rule, check the label on the container or ask the person behind the counter at the paint store before you try to spray any finish.

Spraying equipment

Many of the old-time rules apply to spray guns. For example, you generally get what you pay for. This means that inexpensive vibrator-type spray guns will work in only a limited number of cases. Most of the time they are only strong enough for very thin liquids. The same goes for that attachment for your vacuum cleaner. It will work—sometimes. However, before you go out and spend a lot of money on better equipment, you might try either of these. There's a chance it can do the job.

In most cases, for serious work, you'll have to use a compressor-type spray gun. It has a hose that connects the compressor section to the gun. This is the type that is most commonly used.

There is another type you should know about. It is a pressureless gun, sometimes called a "slinger" by home craftsmen. It works by literally flinging the paint out at such a high speed that it is broken up into tiny, tiny droplets. It is very good for heavier finishes.

For very small occasional jobs, there are spray guns that are powered by carbon dioxide cartridges. These are perfectly fine for small jobs, but they are not suitable for any type of larger-scale finishing work, because they can hold and spray only a small amount of finish at a time.

If pressurized self-spray cans are still sold at the time you are reading this book, you may find them handy and perfectly satisfactory for a great many small jobs about the house. It is expensive to use them, compared to the old-fashioned brush method, but, when you take into account all the fuss and bother of cleanup, you'll probably agree that it's worth the expense for small jobs. Especially since the paint is ready mixed in the proper proportions for spraying.

Working conditions

Proper conditions are important for good results. Ventilation is at the head of the list, for your own comfort as well as for the rapid drying of the finish. Natural ventilation is best, especially if you are spraying any highly flammable materials. If you plan to do a great deal of this kind of work, you might want to invest in a special fan made just for applications where there are vapors that can burn. There should be just enough air current to carry off the excess spray and bring in a constant source of fresh, clean air.

It's also very important that you take all necessary precautions against fire. When flammable finishes are reduced to a fine mist, the fire danger multiplies. For this reason, when you are spraying, don't smoke; and don't work near an open flame. It's just too risky. Even if you are spraying a coating that burns very slowly, the spraying process (transforming the material into a fine mist) is an invitation to potential trouble.

Any time you spray, there's going to be overspray around and on top of the object you're coating. This means you ought to plan on working in an area where the walls can be covered or where they will not be damaged by a few odd layers of paint.

The temperature and humidity are important. For best results, don't try to spray if the temperature is below 65°F.; you won't have as much control, and the finish won't dry properly. This is a general rule; you will find more specific instructions concerning this on the label of the container. It's no use trying to work on humid, muggy days. Few finishes will dry properly under these conditions. Instead, wait for a clear, crisp day with low humidity.

Working out-of-doors is perfectly feasible. Find a spot where you can work in the shade, and make sure you are not surprised by the sun. It can be discouraging to finish coating a piece of furniture only to find that you have miscalculated and the sun, moving in its accustomed orbit, is now beaming directly on your masterpiece. Naturally, a dry day is especially important when working out-of-doors.

It is a good idea to raise the piece of furniture up on a couple of sawhorses or sturdy boxes, rather than to leave it resting on the ground. The force of the spray stirs up dust and dirt. What you are looking for is a smooth finish, not a stucco effect.

If you are working indoors, vacuum the area thoroughly before you start. The air movement of the spray can pluck dust out of surprising corners and deposit it firmly on your newly wet finish. Protect the walls with lightweight plastic drop cloths. You can usually hold these in place with masking tape.

If you have lots of space, you may be able to leave the piece of furniture in one position while you work around it on all sides. Do keep in mind that this generally means that walls have to be protected in every direction. If you are tight on space, you might rig up a crude turntable. Then you can operate the spray equipment from the best vantage point, while you rotate the piece itself to expose different surfaces.

Finally, don't neglect the very basic items of mask and goggles. Hardware stores sell very inexpensive masks designed to cover your nose and mouth so that there is no possibility of breathing in any of the paint or fumes. And to avoid an uncomfortable irritation of your eyes, just wear your goggles.

Using spraying equipment

Almost every finish requires at least some thinning before it can be applied with a spray gun. You'll find information about thinning detailed on the label of the finish itself. The instruction booklet that comes with the particular sprayer you're using will also discuss the subject. Thinning is probably the most important element in achieving a good finish.

In addition to the proper proportion of finish and thinner, make certain you are using the proper thinner. Generally, mineral spirits are used with paint, water with water paint, lacquer thinner with lacquer, et cetera. Again, the label on the container is a gold mine of useful information.

One more thing: Make absolutely certain that there are no lumps in the finish. If you are trying to use up some paint that's been around for a while, this can be a problem. If you see any sign of lumps whatsoever, strain the material through a discarded nylon stocking. Otherwise, the lumps can plug up the spray gun and you'll have to clean it before you can get down to serious work.

Always test the action of your spray gun as well as the finish itself on a piece of scrap wood. The results will give you a pretty good indication as to its capacity. For example, if it spits and won't spray evenly, it's probably too weak for the job. If you can't thin the coating enough so the spray gun can handle it, you might try using heavier equipment. If the finish was heavy, and you did not have good control, you will need more air pressure. Again, you may have to use heavier equipment.

Most spray guns spray out the paint in an oval pattern. You can adjust the pattern so that it's vertical if you're going to spray in a horizontal direction, or horizontal if you are going to spray in vertical bands. Almost all spray guns also have another adjustment for the air pressure. To set this properly, follow the instructions that came with the particular spray gun you are using.

For almost all spray jobs, hold the spray gun six to ten inches away from the surface. This is a general guide, not an absolute rule. Your best bet is to experiment a bit first. When you find the ideal distance for spraying, maintain it precisely throughout the job. If you hold the spray gun too close to the surface, the coating will run and sag, and it will tend to ripple. If you hold the gun too far back, the coating will dry before it hits the surface, causing the finish to be dusty and dull looking.

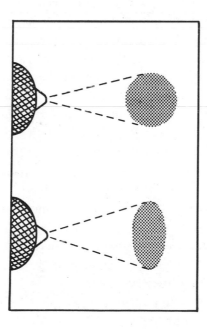

Fig. 40. Adjusting the pattern of the sprayed finish.

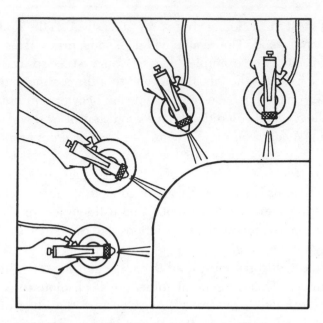

Fig. 41. The correct way to use a spray gun.

There is a definite technique to handling a spray gun. The most common error that amateurs make is to hold the gun in one spot and flick it from side to side by swinging the wrist (like the old Wild West sheriff covering everybody in the saloon). With a spray gun in hand, this is a very bad idea. Instead, move your arm across the work, shifting the angle of your wrist as you go, so the gun stays absolutely perpendicular to the surface at all times. It should always be in the same position, at the same distance.

In most cases, the best technique is to spray in a series of overlapping bands. Tip the gun very slightly so that the excess, or overspray, will be dusted on to an area still to be painted. Then, when you cover that next band, the fresh paint will soften any paint "dust" that's adhering to the surface and absorb it into the finish.

Turn on the spray gun just before you come to the first edge of the surface, and keep it on until you are slightly past the other end. Once again, the purpose here is to give an even coverage and allow the spray gun a split second or so to start operating properly before you start applying finish. It's very important that you spray on an even coat all the way across. You may waste a little paint with this process, but the final finish will be much better.

Overlap the bands by one-third for even coverage. With a little experience you should develop an automatic action as you move across the surface. Start the gun at one side, then move across the surface in a smooth, even motion, keeping the gun exactly the same distance from the surface, and at exactly the same angle at all times. Don't shut it off until you are past the other end of the surface. Spray the next band in the same way, overlapping by one third.

Be sure to allow proper drying time between coats. Once again, this information will be detailed on the label of the container.

Spray at the edge of the corners, so the finish overlaps evenly on either side.

If the nozzle of the spray gun plugs up while you are working, clean it out with a soft, thin object such as a broom straw. The hole that the paint sprays through is a precision opening. If you distort it even slightly, the gun will not work properly. So don't try to clean it with wire.

Some coatings should be scuffed or lightly sanded between coats. This gives a slight roughness or tooth so the next layer will adhere firmly. If this process is required, it will be mentioned on the label. Don't overdo the sanding or scuffing. Light sanding means just that—fine abrasive paper or steel wool with a grade of 320. If sandpaper is

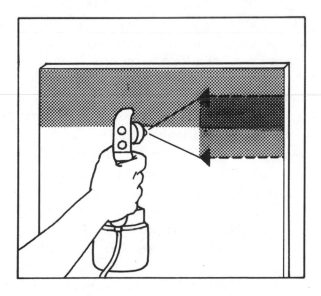

Fig. 42. Spraying in overlapping bands.

called for, use a sanding block. Be very careful when you work on the edges. It is far too easy to cut through in these areas. Remove the dust before applying the next coat.

The best procedure is to build up the finish in a series of thin coats. If you try to do it all in one big layer, the only thing you will get will be a shortcut to gummy disaster. There is nothing more discouraging than a finish that absolutely refuses to dry. Take a bit of extra time and play it safe. Build up the finish slowly, thin layer by thin layer.

Cleanup

Throw out the unused paint as soon as you have finished the job or are stopping for more than a few moments. You may, however, save the paint if it is a decent quality and there's enough to make it worthwhile. Do be sure to mark the container "thinned for spray." Seal it well and identify it thoroughly as to type, color, et cetera. Don't try to save any small amounts that are left over. It is poor economy. Just toss them out.

Self-spray cans

These pressurized containers work in much the same manner as a regular spray gun, but on a smaller scale. However, they do have a tendency to settle and sometimes become gummy if they remain on the shelf too long. For your own protection, buy self-spray paints and finishes from a store that has a lot of turnover.

Most of these containers have an agitator ball (usually a small marble) inside to mix up the coating. To get decent results, it is essential that you shake the container until you can hear the ball rattling around inside. Continue shaking for as long as directed by the instructions on the label, generally two minutes. Do it by the clock. Shaking a can of paint up and down is deadly dull, and under these conditions, two minutes is usually a great deal longer than you think.

In spraying, be sure that you depress the valve on top of the container all the way. There is no intermediate position. It is either all on or all off. The rest of the rules for using self-spray cans are the same as for spray guns.

One technique is different. When you complete the job, or if you stop midway (even for a moment), turn the can upside down and spray

Fig. 43. Cleaning a self-spray can.

until only gas comes out of the nozzle. Then wipe the nozzle off with a clean cloth or a bit of paper. The idea is to clear the internal spray mechanism so that the paint won't clog it inside the can.

If the nozzle itself becomes plugged, pull it off and soak it in the proper solvent for the coating. If necessary, you can clean out the opening in the nozzle with a broom straw.

Read the label very carefully. Manufacturers have gone to a great deal of trouble to formulate the material inside the can, and they have firm ideas about how to use it. In general, they are right. You should take advantage of all this know-how. For example, with some self-spray coatings, the first layer is to be "misted" on. This means the material should be applied as very light fogging. Once this preliminary layer is dry, other coats can be applied "wet." Don't play games. Do exactly what the man says. If you apply a full, wet coat immediately, it may peel off the surface. The misted coat will provide proper adhesion for the following coats.

Self-spray cans come with a built-in problem: Because the paint is mixed with a gas (that's the pressure that sprays it out), if you spray too close to the surface, the gas will have no chance to evaporate before the paint flows out onto the wood. As a result, the gas will bubble up through the coating. If this becomes a problem, the remedy is simple: Put more distance between the spray can and the surface.

Finally, don't punch a hole in the can at any point. Even though it seems to be empty, it may still contain enough gas under pressure to cause an explosion. And don't toss the empty container into an incinerator; the heat may cause it to explode. Always store the cans at room temperature and never leave them on top of the furnace.

QUICK AND EASY FINISHES 12

FURNITURE FINISHING DOES not have to be a long, arduous process. There are tricks, gimmicks, and unusual approaches, as well as some perfectly workable shortcuts. All these can trim the time considerably for a great many finishing jobs. A few words of caution, however.

Most of the time, the finishing schedules listed in this chapter work very well. However, there is an element of unpredictability. You will have better results if you are willing to take a bit of extra time to test. Try the finish first on a bit of scrap wood. Make sure you like the effect you get and that the finish goes on without any problems. Then go to work on the furniture itself.

Again, before you use any of these finishes, the furniture must be clean, free of any old finishes, completely smooth, and, if necessary, bleached, stained, and filled.

Floor finish

This is a clear finish sometimes sold under the name of sealer-coater. It is intended to go on raw wood. Make sure you buy the type that is intended for application with a lamb's wool squeegee.

The application is simplicity itself. Just mop the finish on. Keep applying it until the wood will no longer absorb it and a thin layer remains on the surface. Wait about ten minutes. Then, using lots of soft, clean rags, wipe off the excess finish.

Allow the piece to dry thoroughly—generally, overnight will do. Then apply one or two coats of clear paste wax, buffing vigorously between coats.

Since this particular finish is sturdy enough to protect a surface that is walked on, it can give quite a rugged finish to furniture. Just make sure you are applying it to raw wood. It is designed to seep into the fibers, to toughen and stiffen the wood. If any of the old finish remains in the pores of the wood when furniture has been stripped, the floor finish cannot do its job.

Floor finish plus tinting colors

With this routine, you can get a combination finish and stain merely by adding the proper tinting colors to the finish. It's actually a lot simpler than it sounds. At a paint store, buy tinting colors designed to go into floor finish. The clerk behind the counter can advise you, but for the most part stick to earth colors: raw and burnt sienna and raw and burnt umber. You can get a very interesting variation of wood tones using only these four tones. In any case, stay away from red, even if you are trying to imitate red maple or mahogany. It is an overpowering shade. The same is true for orange.

Making the proper color involves mixing and testing, mixing and testing. When you think you have achieved the exact tone you want, or one perhaps a little bit darker, test it on a piece of scrap wood. The application is the same as for the floor finish. Incidentally, the same caution applies: Use the finish on raw, unfinished and completely clean wood.

For really fine results, when using a floor finish, allow the piece to dry overnight and rub it down with 000 steel wool. Then apply a coat of paste wax and buff it vigorously.

Penetrating resin

This is another easily applied finish that eliminates all worry about brush marks or dust particles settling onto the surface. The completed finish is really tough. It will shrug off wear and is surprisingly difficult to dent. It is impervious to most household chemicals and to alcohol and water.

Penetrating resin gives you a very natural looking finish. Like the floor finish, it is absorbed into the surface itself; it is not a "skin" coating. Although it is sold as a clear finish (you can also buy it in tinted form or mix your own), it will darken the surface slightly. However, this generally enhances the grain of the wood, so most home craftsmen regard it as a plus.

The surface should be prepared as for floor finish. The wood should be smooth and free of dust, and there should be no trace of a prior finish.

Swab on the resin with a cloth pad or wad of 000 steel wool. The idea is to wet the surface and keep it wet for about half an hour. Follow the instructions on the label for the exact timing. If you find the finish drying out in spots, simply swab on a bit more resin. Keep the entire surface evenly wet.

At the end of the soaking period, mop the surface with soft, clean rags. If some of the material works itself out of the pores of the wood and comes to the surface in spots, don't be alarmed; no damage is being done. Merely mop up the little pools.

Fig. 44. Applying penetrating resin with steel wool.

After coating all surfaces, allow the piece to dry for twenty-four hours at room temperature. Then apply the finish again. Three coats with twenty-four hours' drying time between create a lustrous, almost indestructible finish.

Sometimes, when you are applying the second or third layer, the resin will begin to harden on the surface before you have a chance to wipe it up. If this should happen, swab on a bit more of the finish, using a pad of 000 steel wool. This will soften the coating so that you can mop the entire surface dry.

Resin finish comes with one amazing built-in bonus. If, despite its toughness, you do manage to scratch the surface, the repair is easy. Just apply a little more resin, and you'll tone down the scratch until it is hardly noticeable.

Varnish and oil

The procedure sounds most unorthodox, but it works—most of the time. If you have read the section on applying varnish, you know that the one problem is the presence of bubbles. Varnish just seems to invite them. That's why applying it by brush is so tricky. With this system, you don't even use a brush. Here's how it goes.

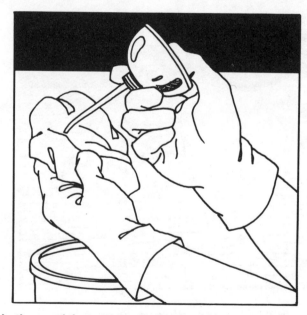

Fig. 45. Apply the varnish and oil with a soft cloth.

Fold up a small wad of soft, lintless cloth; a well-washed handkerchief is fine for this job. Pour one tablespoon of varnish into its center, and add a little liquid oil. Almost any kind of liquid oil—lubricating oil, household oil, sewing machine oil—will do.

Rub this combination into the wood. Keep rubbing until you have literally massaged it into the surface of the wood. If the pad tends to stick at any point, add a bit more oil. If you run out of varnish, add more and some oil to the cloth, as above. Finally, allow the surface to dry thoroughly—about twenty-four hours. Then go over the surface lightly with 000 steel wool.

Apply the second and third coats in the same manner. The final result will be a rich, soft finish. Most of it will be below the surface, with a very thin layer, or skin, on top. Because of the waiting time, this is a fairly long process, but it is the easiest way I know to get a truly lustrous looking varnish finish.

Fabric dye and floor finish

If you would like bright, contemporary shades on your furniture that allow the grain and the natural formation of the wood to show through, this schedule is well worth a try. One warning: Those words of caution advising you to test all finishes on scrap wood before proceeding with any major work go double here. Since you are working with tints and shades intended for fabric rather than wood, there's no way of telling in advance what you are going to get. And of course no way of knowing whether you will like it or not. For example, green wood can be extremely handsome. In a slightly different shade, or in another individual's eyes, ghastly might be a better word. However, in keeping with the title of this chapter, the routine is fast and easy. Either use liquid fabric dye or make a concentrated mixture of the powdered variety. Then start testing. Apply it with a wad of cloth to a piece of scrap that is exactly the same wood as the furniture you are going to finish. If the color is too intense, dilute the fabric dye. Keep working until you get an effect you like.

It is important to apply the dye liberally. Allow it to soak into the wood. If you try to brush it on, you may wind up with uneven tones. Allow the wood to dry thoroughly (probably overnight), and then check the color once more. If you are satisfied with the results, it is time to go to work on the furniture itself.

Because fabric dye is a water stain, it raises the grain on almost all wood. As a result, you will have to smooth the surface lightly when the stain is completely dry. Use 000 steel wool. Just rub a pad of it across the surface to lop off the little "whiskers" of wood that may project up.

Stain alone gives no protection whatsoever to the wood. For this you will have to apply a clear floor finish. Just follow the application instructions I have already given for this material.

Synthetic oil finish

The name is a bit misleading. This material is actually a plastic with oil added. It has several advantages. When applied, it sinks into the wood and builds up to form a deep sealer. There are no problems with brush marks, because you apply it with a cloth. The final effect is a deep patina without any "skin" or any glossy shine. It is especially good for enhancing the grain and tone of the wood itself. However, the finished wood will have only a limited amount of protection; this is not a rough, tough, knockabout finish.

Application is easy. Merely flow on the synthetic oil finish with a cloth, just covering the surface evenly and thoroughly. Allow it to dry (this generally takes overnight) and then smooth it with 000 steel wool. Apply two more coats in the same way.

Heavy plastic

You probably will not be able to buy heavy plastic in a paint or hardware store; it is really a hobby shop item. The final effect is flat, smooth, highly glossy, and completely transparent. However, it is not really as tough as it looks. The surface can be scratched, and sometimes objects merely left on it will mar it. So, although it creates a great effect, it is no substitute for harder finishes.

I have seen some interesting results from this finish. It is especially handsome where the undersurface is extremely rough. For example, on a tabletop made out of weatherbeaten barn wood, this kind of finish might be superb. All the battered wood fibers would show clearly, but the surface would be slick and easily cleaned. For a while one company used this kind of material to finish old hatch covers from World War II

Fig. 46. Making a heavy plastic tabletop.

victory ships. They took battered, beat-up wood and transformed it into very handsome dining room tables.

To use this material, form a lip or dam around the edge of the surface, making certain it is absolutely level. Mix the plastic according to the instructions on the container. It comes as a clear material plus a catalyst, and it doesn't start to harden until the two are mixed together. Pour this mixture onto the surface, carefully working out all bubbles with a pointed stick or wire.

Follow the instructions on the label for the exact drying and setting times. These vary according to the brand of material. You may want to build up the coating in a couple of layers, rather than attempting the job all at once. Work on only one surface at a time.

Although this finish can be used on any piece of furniture, it is best used on tabletops or for transforming any flat surface into a superb tabletop.

Thinned enamel

Enamel thinned to a 50–50 mixture is very easy to apply and dries quickly. This means you can build up several layers in very little time. And since enamel is available in so many attractive colors, this is a very practical way to build up a brightly colored opaque surface.

Use the thinner recommended on the label of the container. Mix the enamel thoroughly, and then pour some of it into another container. Add an equal amount of the thinner to the second container, stir and test. If you have thinned the mixture too much, simply add more enamel.

You can apply this watery mixture with a brush, or you can even flow it on with a cloth. Allow it to dry, then smooth the surface with 000 steel wool.

There are two ways to create a finish. Either apply three or four coats of the thinned enamel, or apply one coat of thinned enamel and one coat of regular enamel in the same color. The final look is the same.

Plywood sealer

If you have ever worked with fir plywood, you know that it's almost impossible to paint it. Because the wild fir grain bleeds through almost anything, a special finish was developed just for fir plywood. It is a heavy-duty sealer that blocks off the dark grain formation so that a light finish will go evenly on top. This same material makes a perfectly fine furniture finish for other types of wood.

Add tinting colors (get the proper ones from the person behind the counter at the paint store) and mix the tone or shade that you like. As I mentioned before, work with a limited pallette: burnt and raw umber plus burnt and raw sienna. One or a combination of these gives you a surprisingly wide choice of tones and tints. Try out the color on scrap wood.

When you get a color you like, apply it to the surface of the wood. Flow it on with a brush or a wad of cloth. Use a liberal amount of sealer, although not so much as required for floor finish. Build up one or two layers, allowing proper drying time between applications. Finish with one coat of clear floor finish (not the penetrating variety; use the urethane type).

Fake hand-rubbed oil finish

This finish gives a sense of Old World craftsmanship. When you rub your hand across the surface, you can feel the wood grain and the very slight drag that is the mark of a genuine hand-rubbed oil finish.

Here's how to do it. Merely use any one of the several finishing procedures already detailed in this book. Penetrating sealer is ideal, as is floor finish or penetrating resin. After the last coat is completely dry, rub some boiled linseed oil onto the surface. Work it back and forth with the palms of your hands, and then rub off the excess with a soft cloth. With this easy bit of fakery, you'll get the aroma and the feel of a true cabinetmaker's finish.

Just one bit of caution. The finish must be absolutely dry before the linseed oil goes on. If necessary, wait four or five days or even a week after applying the last bit of the true finish. Also make sure that you use boiled linseed oil; there's another variety that never seems to dry.

CREATING AN ANTIQUE FINISH 13

DISTRESSING FOR SIMULATING AGE

THERE IS AN OLD Vermont fable about a backwoods character who used to turn out fake antiques. According to legend, he would take a brand-new piece of reproduction furniture into the backyard, blast it with birdshot, beat it with a tire chain, and soak it in the pond for a week. Then he would clean it off and sell it to some unsuspecting tourist as a genuine antique.

You can be sure of just one thing: That story is fable and nothing more. No one would buy that kind of obvious fakery. Truly effective distressing involves battering with a gentle hand. Shotguns and tire chains are far too obvious. For the rest of its life that particular piece of furniture would always scream "fraud."

Let's backtrack for a bit and consider the basic philosophy behind the whole procedure of distressing. What are we trying to do? Quite simply, it is this: We are seeking to simulate the marks of true age. People don't live in a vacuum, and their furniture reflects their way of life and also the use that each piece has had. For example, one would expect to find a burn mark on the shelf of a pipe cabinet. A series of scratch marks might logically be etched into the side of a candle box hanging next to a table. All the marks of age and use have a direct relationship to the utilization of each specific piece of furniture. The overall idea is to simulate the marks of age and the signs of day-to-day use in a normal household. If you started out with a nicely finished piece of fine furniture, clobbering it with a tire chain would serve no purpose. You would add fraudulent distress marks which that particular piece of furniture would never have gotten.

For the most part, you will get best results working with raw wood. To start, confine your efforts to unfinished pieces of pine or other soft woods. Stores and mail order catalogs abound with these. You can even get them in the shape of reproduction antiques: tables, benches, chairs, chests, et cetera. Keep in mind, however, that the precaution about a gentle touch goes double with this wood. Because it is soft, there is danger of distressing it beyond the point of credibility.

How to distress

Select your tools from this armory: (a) A bunch of old keys, the kind that were used for the back door or the kitchen door. These are straight, with a loop at one end and a slightly cut out raised portion at the other. String six or eight of these loosely on a one-foot length of cord. (b) An old, chipped grinding wheel. If you can't find a chipped one, hack a few pieces out of the rim yourself. (c) An irregular S-shaped piece of hard wire. Piano wire is fine. You can make a couple of these if you like. The upper loop should be a different size from the lower one. (d) Some old shellac. (e) A wood rasp or a coarse file. (f) A ball peen hammer. (g) A fist-sized bundle of nails, all pointing in one direction and held together with a stout rubber band around the middle.

How do you use this interesting assortment?

Try flailing the keys. Hold them by the cord and wham them down onto the surface of the wood. Because they will constantly shift in position, you will get an irregular pattern of tiny dents.

Slip a short length of dowel through the center of the grinding wheel. With a hand on either end of the dowel, press down with as much force as you can muster while you roll the wheel across the surface. The chipped sections will make different kinds of marks. Because the chips are strung out along the rim of the wheel, the marks won't be repeated often enough to be noticeable.

Lay the S-shaped pieces of wire against the surface of the wood and

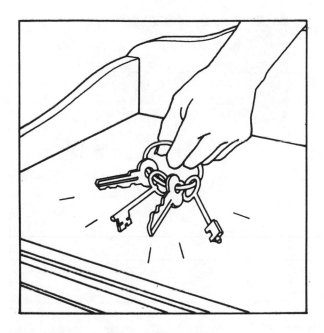

Fig. 47. Flailing the keys to distress the surface.

Fig. 48. Using the grinding wheel.

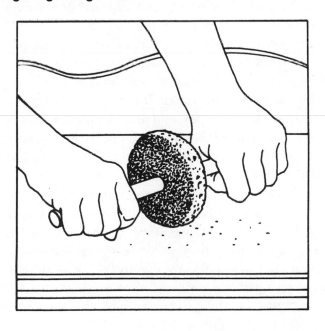

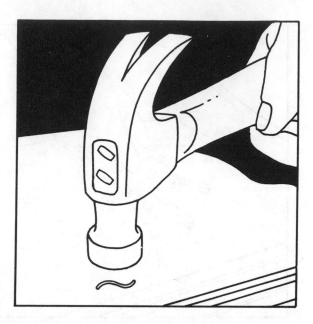

Fig. 49. Imitating furniture worms with S-shaped pieces of wire.

give them a firm tap with a hammer. The idea is to imitate the little marks of worms that sometimes get into wood. Use a great deal of discretion with this technique, so it won't appear that the piece is overrun with termites.

Bang the surface a few times with the ball peen end of the hammer. Don't get carried away. It is not often in any household that something big and heavy falls on the furniture and dents it.

Use the rasp or file to round all corners and edges. Any piece of furniture that's been around for a hundred years or so has been handled and polished. This kind of friction alone generally means that there are no sharp edges left. Everything is at least slightly rounded.

After this, back off a bit and look at the piece of furniture. If it is a chair, for example, try to figure out where it would show the most wear in normal use. People probably tipped the chair back at an angle and then propped their feet up on one of the rungs. Generally, then, the top front surfaces of the rungs become flattened. So flatten them with the file. Also figure out where the back of the chair would get a little battered from contact with the wall, and work on this spot slightly with the rasp. The greatest wear always occurs where the piece is handled, and this is what you want to imitate.

Fig. 50. Bouncing the bundle of nails.

Only one burn mark is permitted per piece of furniture. Pour a small puddle of shellac onto the surface where you want to create the burn mark. Again, keep your expansive nature well in hand. A puddle about the size of a quarter will do fine. Touch a match to this and let it burn away completely.

Hold the bundle of nails in your hand and bounce them down onto the wood surface. Again, exercise restraint. You are not trying to create a polka-dot effect.

One more technique: If the piece has any hardware already mounted in place, keep a wet cloth over it for a few days. This should make the metal rust, and the rust stains discolor the surrounding wood.

The final true secret

The treatments I have just described are merely the first stage. I am now going to tell you about a simple, direct process that will make all of your work look astoundingly authentic: With sandpaper and 180 steel wool, remove about seventy-five percent of the damage you have done. In normal usage, mars, scratches, stains and wear are not left raw on the surface. When damage occurs, people generally try to cover it up, to soften it. That's precisely what you should do, just as if you are appalled at what has happened to this nice piece of furniture and must do your very best to make it presentable. In the process you will wind up with a subtle effect that will look more real than the results of the smashing and battering you have done.

Hardware

If you can salvage some old or antique hardware, good. If not, it is relatively simple to simulate the look of old-time hand-wrought hinges and hasps.

For example, pieces of antique furniture had butterfly-shaped hinges that fastened onto the surface. It is not too hard to make such hinges out of ordinary butt hinges. Saw the butterfly shape out of the metal, and then grind the outer edges on an abrasive wheel until they are relatively thin. Place the hinge flat on a piece of paper and spray it with one coat of black paint. Dribble fine sawdust lightly on the surface and spray on a second coat of black paint. This will give the slightly uneven effect of hand-wrought metal.

As an alternate method, you can cut a fake hinge out of old sheet lead and attach it to a regular hinge. Cut out the two segments of the butterfly shape and beat them lightly with a ball peen hammer to create a hammered effect. Paint the metal black and fasten it on top of the regular hinge leaves.

Nails

Old-time cabinetmakers, especially those who built the pine-country pieces, fastened hardware in place with nails clinched in the back. Screws were very difficult to make because each one had to be filed out by hand, so they were used only on the very fine furniture, and even then quite sparingly. Some specialty building supply companies sell reproduction antique nails. If you have trouble locating these, however, it is not too difficult to make your own.

To make imitation hand-wrought nails, use horseshoe nails or the smaller size called pony nails. These have a long tapered shank and a relatively thick head. Because the head is fairly soft, it can be battered into the shape you want.

Clamp the pony nail in a vise, holding it firmly just under the head. Pound straight down on the head to flatten it, and finish off the job by clobbering the head from each of four sides to form a rosette.

To fasten this hardware in place, drive the pony nail through the hole in the hinge and through the wood underneath until the head of the nail rests flush against the hinge. Clinch the shank of the nail by giving it two bends with a pair of pliers, one right at the point where it comes through the wood and the other about a half inch from the end. To embed the turned-under shank of the nail in the wood, hold one hammer against the head of the nail while you clobber the back surface with the other.

All of these techniques will really work only on what is considered Early American furniture. For the European furniture or the finer, more expensive pieces of American furniture, effects should be much more subtle. After all, because the owners had spent a great deal of money on the furniture, and were proud of it and well aware of its value even then, it was almost always well cared for.

Distressing on this type of furniture, therefore, must be far more subtle. As a matter of fact, most of it is done in the finish rather than in the surface of the wood. This means that tiny little flecks of black in the form of little teardrops are carefully applied to the finish with a paintbrush. Any imitation repairs should be done with exquisite craftsmanship. There might be, for example, one patch in an unobtrusive place, made with a wood that comes very close but does not quite match the color and grain of the original lumber. There might be one indiscretion, such as a dark ring left by a glass. This can be simulated by dipping the base of a glass into black dye and applying it to the surface like a cookie cutter.

In general, the same overall rules apply. Use a gentle hand and a wild imagination.

ANTIQUE FINISHES

The following suggestions are extremely interesting and mostly unusual approaches to furniture finishing. They are not, however, guaranteed to be successful in every case. As before, try out any finish on some wood that is the same as that used on the furniture you are going to finish. Then you will know what the effect is going to be. If you like it, great. It is time to go to work. If not, try another finish, or shift the pigmentation a bit. Even the process of experimenting to find what you really like is a great deal of fun.

Authentic reproduction finish

It was not only tradition that said that a barn should be painted red. In reality, red was the cheapest dark pigment that a cost-conscious farmer could buy; red was also attractive and hid the stains of time. So barns were nearly always painted red. Because it was a tint that the farmer had around the farmhouse, he tended to use it wherever he could for furniture.

Even today a lucky antique hunter will be stripping down a piece of furniture picked up in a backwoods farmhouse and suddenly let out a scream. He has removed all of the more recently applied layers of paint and has reached a final layer of flint-hard barn-red paint. It is impossible to remove it except by scraping, and even then, inevitably, some of it will be left behind in the pores of the wood. So, when the new finish is applied, there will be a slight undercurrent of barn red.

The purpose of this particular finish is to give that precise effect: that the furniture has at one time been painted with barn paint; it has been scraped off, but a bit of it still remains.

You can buy regular barn paint from any of the large mail order houses as well as from some paint stores. Do not mix it. Pour off the liquid from the top and save it. Then stir the remaining thick portion in the bottom of the bucket. Add back just enough of the liquid to make a loose paste. Apply the mixture to your furniture with a wad of cloth and allow it to sit for fifteen to twenty minutes. Wipe off the excess. Allow the surface to dry and then apply several coats of a clear finish.

Chewing tobacco

That is correct. This was once used as a stain or coloration for furniture. Buy a wad or bag of chewing tobacco, the cheaper the better. Stuff it into a glass jar and pour denatured alcohol on top. Allow the mess to sit for hours, days, weeks—it doesn't much matter. The idea is just to draw out as much of the coloration from the tobacco as possible.

Pour off the liquid and test it for color on a piece of scrap wood. If the effect is not dark enough, allow the alcohol to evaporate until the liquid is more concentrated. If it is too dark, add more alcohol.

When applied to pine furniture, this stain will raise the grain slightly. After the wood is completely dry, smooth it with 000 steel wool. For a dull finish, apply penetrating sealer. If you want a skin on the surface, use a clear finish; for a soft effect, use a buffed wax finish.

Country glazing

Country glazing is a two-coat process. It consists of a background color (generally light beige or white) with a darker tone on top. Here is the procedure.

Use any good standard enamel for the background shade. To apply, just follow the instructions on the label. Allow the finished surface to dry thoroughly. When it is completely hard, lightly smooth the surface with 000 steel wool. Wipe off any traces of dust.

Apply the glaze, or second coating. This is generally a gray, brown, or grayish-brown tone. The color should be selected to simulate the effect of built-up polish, age, and dust embedded in the surface. Incidentally, you can buy a kit of ground color and glaze in many paint stores. Just ask for a glazing kit, and pick out the specific colors you like. If you do not buy a kit, ask for wiping glaze and, again, choose the color that appeals to you. Do remember that very little of it is going to remain on the surface of the piece, however.

Brush on the glaze and let it stand for the length of time called for on the label, generally about ten minutes. Then wipe it off. The whole effect of antiquing is achieved in this one wiping process. The idea is to leave some color in the crevices and inside corners but almost none in the center of flat surfaces. The difference must be gradual. In this way you can simulate the years of polishing, years of use when open areas were rubbed and exposed to friction.

In some cases you may want to apply one coat of a dull finish on top of the final glazing to protect it.

Highlighting

Highlighting is similar to country glazing, but it permits the grain and texture of the wood to show through. Instead of using a solid color base or ground coat, use any of the relatively clear or transparent

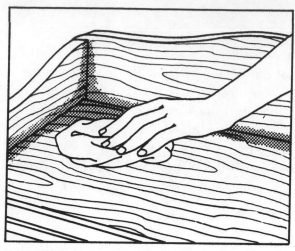

Fig. 51. Wiping off the glaze.

finishes previously described. For the top or highlighting coat, use a wiping glaze that is lighter in overall tone than the country glaze. You will probably find that a sort of earth/amber tone works well, and you can get this by mixing a bit of burnt umber color into a light-toned wiping glaze.

The application procedure is much the same as that described in country glazing, except that you will have to be a bit more diligent about wiping away the top coating from the areas that you want to remain clear. In this routine, the wood tone and grain readily show through where the glaze has been thoroughly wiped away, and they are subdued in the inaccessible and unwiped areas.

Barn wood

The best treatment for weathered barn siding is to leave it alone. It already has as much antiquing as wood can take. Anything you add will generally make it look less authentic. However, if you are finicky, the wood can be sprayed with a dull-finish clear lacquer. By the same token, if you want to build up a usable surface without the crevices that are part and parcel of barn siding, you may want to use the clear plastic coating described on page 142.

There are all sorts of cute techniques advocated for imitating antique effects, such as knotholes made by dipping your thumb in paint and then applying the paint to the surface with a swirl. If you are tempted to try such horrors, use large amounts of restraint. The effect looks as phony as it sounds.

COVER-UP FINISHES 14

NONE OF THE PROCEDURES in this chapter are really furniture finishes, at least not in the sense that they are applied with a brush, roller or swab. However, they do cover the surface of the wood and generally produce rather handsome effects. This being the case, you might consider adding them to your repertoire of furniture finishes. One precaution: It is almost impossible to remove them, once they have been applied.

In all instances cover-up finishes are designed for smooth wood surfaces. That means the furniture has been sanded and dusted.

Plastic laminate (Including Formica and Micarta)

First cut the plastic sheet to size. It should be about 1/16 inch larger overall so that you can later trim and bevel the outer edges. If you are cutting inside openings, such as one for a sink, cut them to the exact size in most cases. A sink rim or similar fitting usually hides the edge of the plastic laminate sheet. Cut all the openings before you cement down the sheet, including holes that you might need for pipes or faucets.

Apply contact cement to both surfaces, the furniture and the underside of the plastic sheet. Contact cement is a treacherous material. As the name indicates, this adhesive bonds instantly on contact. There is absolutely no chance to lift the sheet and try again once the glue has taken hold. Follow the instructions on the label of the adhesive container, and allow the surfaces to dry thoroughly.

Put a series of slip sheets on the top of the furniture surface. These are nothing more than strips of paper slightly overlapped. They give you a chance to jockey the plastic sheet into exact position before the glue removes your options.

Place the plastic sheet on the furniture and shift it until it is in perfect position. Position a strip of wood on top of the sheet at one edge and clamp it down to hold the entire sheet exactly in position. Lift the loose end of the plastic sheet and slide out the first paper strip.

Carefully press down the plastic sheet. It will bond instantly in the spot where the paper was removed. Take off the clamp, lift the rest of the sheet slightly, and slide out the rest of the paper strips. Starting at the strip already bonded, bow the sheet slightly in a downward curve and gradually press it down. After the sheet is in position, pound the surface with a rubber mallet so that it bonds perfectly across the entire surface.

Smooth and bevel any exposed edges, using a file or the special attachment designed to go onto a quarter-inch drill. Trim molding, avail-

Fig. 52. Positioning a plastic sheet with slip sheets.

able in most hardware stores and lumberyards, clamps into place on the edge of the furniture to conceal the joint if you prefer that effect.

Wallpaper

Considering the variety of colors and patterns available through wallpaper stores, it is amazing that wallpaper it not used more often for furniture finishing. You can get an especially attractive effect by matching fabric and wallpaper; many stores sell these coordinates. For example, you may want to make a dust ruffle for a dressing table out of fabric and use the matching pattern for the top of the piece.

After smoothing the furniture completely, seal the wood with two coats of glue sizing or shellac. Sand the surface lightly with a sanding block, and clean up carefully. Any little fibers of wood left behind will show up in the surface of the wallpaper, so dust the surface thoroughly to remove the last particle of wood or shellac. Then apply a coat of vinyl paste to the back of the wallpaper strip.

Place the wallpaper on the top of the table and brush it down firmly, using a standard wallpaper smoothing brush. Trim the paper

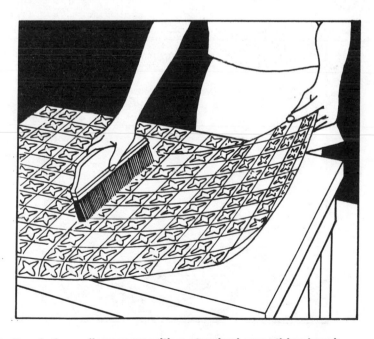

Fig. 53. Brush the wallpaper on with a standard smoothing brush.

along the edge of the tabletop, using a sharp razor blade. Wipe off any excess paste that oozes out, and allow the surface to dry completely.

Finish the job by applying several coats of clear lacquer or clear plastic finish for a durable surface.

Gasket cork

Automotive supply stores sell cork in sheet form, as it is used by mechanics to cut out gaskets. But it also makes a very interesting and handsome tabletop.

Brush a coat of white glue over the entire surface of the tabletop. Press down the cork, rolling it out lightly with your hands as you go. If you have to butt two strips of cork together to cover the surface, first allow them to overlap, and then cut through both layers at the midpoint of the overlap. Peel off and discard the excess, and carefully press the two edges together.

Use a rolling pin over the entire surface to remove all traces of air bubbles. Allow the cork sheet to dry thoroughly, and then trim it along the edges. As with the wallpaper, coat the surface with a layer or two of clear plastic.

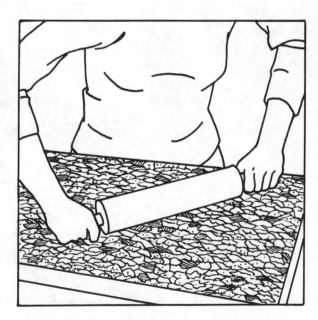

Fig. 54. Use a rolling pin to smooth the cork and to remove air bubbles.

Fabric

As long as you follow these instructions, you should have no trouble in covering a surface with fabric. Choose any design or pattern that appeals to you, but remember that not all fabrics can be used for this purpose. They must be thin, tightly woven and smooth. In general, thin printed cottons work much better than coarse, open-weave fabrics.

Start the job by applying sizing or spray starch to the back of the fabric. Trim the fabric to approximate size and iron it carefully. Do not fold it after you have ironed it.

Dilute white glue with water until it is the consistency of paint. Brush a coat of it onto the furniture and apply the fabric immediately. Brush the fabric flat, using a standard wallpaper smoothing brush. Allow the surface to dry completely.

Trim the fabric to exact size with a razor blade. Then coat the surface with clear lacquer or plastic.

Adhesive plastic

Adhesive plastic is now available in hardware and dime stores under several different brand names. It is sold by the yard and is available in a wide variety of colors and patterns.

To apply it, first trim it to approximate size. Then remove a little strip of the protective paper from the adhesive at one end of the piece. Position the plastic, but be careful not to press down the little strip of exposed adhesive. When you have the material in place, hold it there by smoothing the exposed adhesive against the tabletop.

Start to peel the protective paper off of the rest of the adhesive underneath. Carefully smooth the plastic into place against the surface as you remove the paper. When the entire length has been pressed down, use a rubber roller or a rolling pin to roll out the bubbles. If any bubbles get trapped under the surface, pierce the plastic with a pin to remove them, while you roll the surface once more. Finally, trim the plastic along the edges of the surface.

General rules for other materials

Most of the suggestions here are just that—suggestions. There is no reason why you can't experiment with other materials to cover the surfaces of furniture. To guide you in your project, here are a few helpful rules.

If you are putting down a material that is porous, be sure to seal it so that the adhesive does not seep through.

Use an adhesive that is compatible with both the covering and the top surface.

Apply the adhesive according to the manufacturer's instructions. If you have to thin it, use the recommended thinner.

Use a compatible coating, such as clear lacquer or plastic, for the protective layer.

Obviously you are limited only by your imagination. If you are looking for suggestions, try cementing down such diverse materials as posters, large photos or foreign newspapers. Or make a collage out of match folders, wine bottle labels, or an accumulation of the kids' report cards.

NOVELTY FINISHES 15

SOME PEOPLE CALL THEM fun finishes, which is not a bad term, really. For the most part they are unusual effects. Used sparingly (sometimes with a sense of humor), they can be quite effective. In this chapter you will find some tricks, gimmicks, and special effects that are also fun to do.

Spatter finish

This is great when the kids want to participate. From a practical standpoint, spatter finish has one unexpected advantage. It is the best cover-up you can devise. It will hide a patched floor, unevenness, waviness, and stains. It is also bright and cheerful. The prime disadvantage is that any small object dropped onto a spatter-finished surface immediately becomes invisible.

Start by applying a base coat. In most cases this will be an enamel of some kind. Follow the standard procedure for applying this material. The final surface should be completely dry and smooth.

There are two ways to create the spatters. For the first method, dunk the bristles of a brush lightly into the paint and then hit the brush

Fig. 55. Creating spatters by striking a brush against a stick

Fig. 56. . . . and by rubbing a stick against a brush.

against a stick held in your other hand. The paint will flick off the end of the bristles and spatter down onto the surface. Incidentally, you are not restricted to one-color spatters; multi-hued effects can be quite nice too.

The other technique involves using a stiff-bristled brush. For small surfaces, a toothbrush will do. Again dip the bristles in paint. This time rub a stick against the bristles, so that they are pulled back and then flipped forward. This will spray tiny droplets onto the surface. When you have a spatter effect that you like, allow it to dry completely, and then apply several layers of a clear top coating.

As a variation on this same procedure, you can try dribbling strings of paint with a few well-placed blobs, à la Jackson Pollock. Art it may not be, but isn't artistic good enough?

Stencil

Stenciling is a traditional technique that, properly followed, can be just as effective today as it was a hundred years ago. The old Hitchcock chairs, much sought after by collectors, were frequently decorated by this technique.

First, cut the stencil out of sturdy brown wrapping paper. It can be one you designed yourself or a commercially made one. Apply black shellac to the surface to be stenciled. The job may require two or three coats, with proper drying time between. The final surface should be hard, smooth, and solid black. It should also have a very slight tack, which means that you will have to do the stenciling before the final layer has dried completely.

Position the stencil. Use gold powder as pigment; pick some up with your thumb and finger and carefully pat it through the openings of the stencil. When you have covered the entire surface, remove the stencil carefully. Allow the stenciling to dry and then protect it with one or two coats of clear finish.

If this old-fashioned method sounds like too much work, you can get a similar effect with a can of spray paint in gold, silver, or any other color you choose. In this case, we make a slightly larger frame for the stencil to protect the rest of the chair from over-spray.

The main problem with the spray technique is that the paint tends to drift under the edges of the stencil. To prevent this, cut the stencil out of the adhesive-backed plastic material discussed as a cover-up finish in the previous chapter. Make sure the final coat of background paint is completely dry and hard with no tack; then peel the backing off the plastic and press it into position. Because it is possible to seal all of the edges, you will be able to spray a pattern and leave a sharp, clean line around it when you peel off the stencil.

Decals

When I was a child, decals were known as cockamamies. The patterns have been updated, but the method of application has remained the same.

The surface should be smooth, hard, and dry. Soak the decal in water until it becomes loosened from the paper backing. Slide the decal from the paper directly onto the surface, and smooth it down carefully. Brush or spray on one or two coats of clear finish to protect the surface.

Pickled or limed finish

A pickled finish is only effective on woods which have open grain. Oak is generally used. In fact, many people think of limed oak as a wood, rather than a finish.

Do not apply conventional filler. The idea is to utilize the depressions in the grain, not conceal them. Use silver or white filler; you can buy this ready mixed, or make your own by combining regular filler and pigment.

Apply the tinted filler, allow it to set, wipe off the excess, and let the surface dry thoroughly. This is the standard procedure described in chapter 8.

Finish the job by applying transparent coating. You will probably need two or three coats to build enough "skin" on the surface. As an alternate procedure, you can sometimes use paint in a contrasting color, instead of filler. Just rub it on with a wad of cloth, and wipe it off. The disadvantage to this (or maybe the advantage, depending on how you look at it) is that the grain of the wood—the flow and texture of it—will still be evident.

Ebony luster

This finish has had an interesting past. At various times when furniture styles were very stark, ebony finishes were much in vogue. When public taste wanted a softer effect, ebony luster disappeared for a while. But it keeps being rediscovered.

In earlier times, black shellac was used for this type of finish. Now, however, you can get a slicker, shinier, harder effect with black lacquer. Spray or brush it on in a series of thin coats. When each layer is completely dry, smooth it with 000 steel wool, then dust it carefully. Allow the last coat to dry without the steel wool treatment.

Multicolor flecked paint

This one is easy. The secret is in the paint. Just buy flecked paint at your local store and spray it on, following the instructions on the label. This is a great material for covering up drab furniture or for providing a colorful, carefree finish for casual living.

Textured finish

There are two ways to get a textured finish. Many large paint stores sell textured coating that is ready to apply. The only drawback is that you have to stir it very frequently while you are using it, because the little granules that have been added tend to settle to the bottom. This is not a coating you can apply with a spray gun; it is definitely brushwork.

The alternate procedure is to mix your own. This is comparatively easy, although it does take a bit of experimentation. Just dump some granulated material (most people use cornmeal) into a can of paint. Mix thoroughly and apply with a brush.

If you want to add additional texture or pattern, stipple the surface with a sponge or a wad of crumpled newspaper before the coating has dried completely.

Fig. 57. Stippling with newspaper for a textured finish.

Wrinkle effect

Like the glaze finish discussed in chapter 13, this is a two-coat process. Apply a ground coat or base color. The second coat generally contrasts sharply with the ground coat. For example, if the ground coat is white, you may want to use brown or blue for a second coat. Then again, you may prefer the reverse.

When the ground coat is completely dry, crumple some newspaper into a ball and touch the ball lightly with a paintbrush dipped in the contrasting paint. Then bounce the wad of newspapers against the surface. Repeat this until you get the effect you want. Allow the second layer of paint to dry thoroughly. Then brush or spray on a clear coating to protect the finish.

Marbleizing

The only trick for this finish is knowing what to ask for. Most large paint stores sell a ready-mixed marbleized paint that sprays out fine "veins" of color. You can get this in various color combinations. Merely spray it onto the surface and allow it to dry thoroughly. Then protect the final effect with one or two coats of clear finish.

Super-grain plywood

One of the big problems for home craftsmen is treating fir plywood so that the grain does not "bloom." Ordinarily, virtually any finish you put on fir plywood accentuates the grain. That is why there are all sorts of so-called grain tamers to minimize this bloom. As a reverse twist, it is sometimes fun to accentuate the grain. You wind up with a very striking sort of zebra effect.

In order for this technique to work, you have to use fir plywood. Saturate the surface with an aniline dye of any color you like. Allow it to set for a few minutes and then wipe off the excess. When the wood is completely dry, sand with a sanding block and fine sandpaper. Work back and forth to remove the dye from the raised portions of the grain pattern. Dust the wood surface thoroughly and apply two coats of clear finish.

Grained finish

In many respects grained finish is similar to a glazed finish. It is a two-coat process which requires a bit of artistry on your part.

Start the job by applying a base coat of paint. Because the base and the graining must contrast, plan to use a light ground or base coat, with a darker graining material on top. Following standard procedure, apply one or two coats of the base and allow them to dry until completely hard.

Brush on the graining paint and allow it to partially set. This timing is generally detailed pretty thoroughly on the label.

Now comes the fun part. Make a series of swirls and simulated grain patterns by drawing a graining comb through the still-soft top layer. Professional artisans use a special graining tool for this job. This is an inexpensive gadget that you can buy at most large paint stores. If you don't have one, you can use a pocket comb, a saw blade or any other similar object.

The final effect can range anywhere from a startlingly realistic wood grain to a fanciful pattern that no tree in this world could ever produce.

Fig. 58. Creating wood grain with a comb.

Unless you have a flair for this type of activity, it is best to do some practicing before tackling a major furniture project. If you make a serious mistake, however, you can usually wipe off the top graining coating with a solvent recommended by the manufacturer. Protect the grained surface with one or two layers of a transparent coating.

Incidentally, you can buy kits of graining colors in many large paint stores. They contain the base coat plus the graining color and frequently include some simple graining tools along with complete instructions.

INDEX